ENGLISH PRONUNCIATION
FROM THE FIFTEENTH TO THE
EIGHTEENTH CENTURY

ENGLISH PRONUNCIATION

FROM THE FIFTEENTH TO THE EIGHTEENTH CENTURY

A HANDBOOK TO THE STUDY OF HISTORICAL GRAMMAR

SELECTED AND EDITED BY

CONSTANCE DAVIES, B.A., PH.D. (LOND.)

*Late Lecturer in English Language and Literature in the
University of Reading*

Editor of 'English Literary Prose in the Making'

GREENWOOD PRESS, PUBLISHERS
WESTPORT, CONNECTICUT

This book was catalogued by the Library of Congress as follows:

Bullock-Davies, Constance, *comp.*
   English pronunciation from the fifteenth to the eighteenth
century; a handbook to the study of historical grammar.
Selected and edited by Constance Davies. Westport, Conn.,
Greenwood Press ₍1970₎

   xiii, 167 p.   23 cm.

   Reprint of the 1934 ed.

   1. English language—Pronunciation. 2. English language—Grammar, Historical.   I. Title.

PE1137.B79   1970   421'.52   75–109726
ISBN 0–8371–4216–4   MARC

Library of Congress   71 ₍7₎

Originally published in 1934
by J. M. Dent & Sons, Ltd., London

First Greenwood Reprinting 1970
Second Greenwood Reprinting 1973

Library of Congress Catalogue Card Number 75-109726

ISBN 0-8371-4216-4

Printed in the United States of America

CONTENTS

v

ACKNOWLEDGMENT

My thanks are due to Messrs. Longmans Green and Co., Ltd., for their kind permission to print extracts from the *Memoirs of the Verney Family*.

C. D.

INTRODUCTION

MY aim in making this handbook has been to provide the beginner in historical grammar with a suitable body of first-hand material to serve him as an interesting and intelligible introduction to his subject. The exigencies of modern philological study are such that detailed illustration of the type a young student needs is impossible in the highly technical works that at present constitute his only textbooks; for it is with philology as with every new science, the results of expert research and scholarship take the field first, and it is only after these have been accepted and assimilated that the beginner is considered and his needs provided for. These though few are explicit, being chiefly concerned with the statement of rudiments and their illustration, and the latter is particularly necessary in philology, seeing that the study depends almost entirely on documentary evidence; but where the expert uses only a few of the many examples to his hand, the beginner needs a multiplicity of them, as well to gain acquaintance with first principles as to verify and confirm them. The following extracts, drawn from a number of the most representative documents, will, I hope, supply both needs: they have been chosen expressly to illustrate the chief vowel and consonant changes that have taken place in colloquial English from the fifteenth to the eighteenth century, and at the same time offer abundant corroboration of the phonological developments already traced and established by authoritative historians. There is, however, a further interest attached to a collection of this kind; it indicates more clearly than is perhaps possible in any other way the steady development of speech despite seeming vagaries due to education and taste, and furthermore shows from the philological point of view how written language is dependent upon a perpetual aggregation of personal habits, which at first sight bear the look of idiosyncrasies, but which on closer inspection are seen to be an integral part of a general development which it is the historian's business to rationalize in terms of linguistic science.

It is a commonplace of linguistic history that pronunciation is never static. Whether one regards it from the standpoint of racial groups, dialects, or individual speech, in one's own time, or in time-sequence from early ages, it is always found to possess a variability that practically defies classification. The reason for this is not far to seek; the child imitates as far as it can the speech it hears around it; its acquisition of language is a matter of physical effort, and it necessarily makes several attempts before it reproduces the sounds it hears to its own auditory satisfaction. That it never reproduces them accurately goes without saying, but it thinks it does, and having reached that point ceases to attempt further correction in itself. Herein lies the germ of phonetic change; the parent uses a set of phonemes that is both individual in itself and also characteristic of the group to which it belongs, e.g. class or dialect, and this the child endeavours to acquire, but the result of his efforts is the creation of a new set of individual phonemes of that particular group kind. This process, being operative in every individual, naturally affects all speech groups, from the smallest to the largest, and is thus the root cause of continual change in the phonetic system; and since the change is both regular and constant, because coincident with the recurring factors of birth and death, the face as it were of the language gradually changes completely, Old English merges into Middle English, Middle English into New English.

The unit of variation, then, is the individual. No two men speak exactly alike. As members of a given group they appear to—two Frenchmen speak French, two Yorkshiremen Yorkshire, two brothers like each other—and yet each pronounces his words with some degree of radical difference as a result of his own personality. At the same time each group maintains within itself a phonetic equilibrium, that serves to distinguish it from all others, language from language, dialect from Standard, and so on. The fundamental principle in every case is one and the same, and depends on the slight, unconscious readjustment of individual phonemes within the group to conform as far as possible to the ever-changing group-standard or norm; but since every individual has his own set this group norm is in essence only an abstract average; the apparent uniformity is really the result of an aggregate of approximations.

In this way the sands are forever shifting, although it is only after a long time that the movement alters their whole surface. Looking back over the centuries we can more easily distinguish the changes our ancestors made in the phonetic system than those being made by ourselves, as extension in time is necessary to compute results in speech development; the changes must have been completed before their importance can be assessed. Something of this necessary panoramic view has been supplied in the following extracts; they range over a period of three centuries, and offer considerable evidence for the major changes that occurred during the Early Modern period, especially the Great Vowel Shift, and the less definable but none the less important consonantal changes; but the phonetic significance of them can only be apparent when full stock has been taken of the way in which the spelling symbols were used.

Once a new pronunciation has penetrated colloquial speech there arises a need for a new symbolical representation of it. No matter how unphonetic a system of spelling may be, it possesses phonetic significance in the minds of its users, and any new and accepted pronunciation can be and often is spelt in terms of it. 'Good' or 'correct' spelling is in this sense the symbolic norm for the group as Received Standard pronunciation is the phonetic one. Ideally there should be as many symbols as there are individual pronunciations, but this being impossible if communication is to be maintained, every race has reduced its set of symbols to the intelligible minimum. Spelling is essentially a medium; in itself it is not of primary importance. Any system will suit the average man's needs as long as the other fellow understands it. It is only when we have to study speech historically that the symbols seem inadequate or perverse, and our attitude in this is largely a projection into the past of our present difficulties; the sense of inadequacy is entirely due to our attempt to resuscitate an admittedly ephemeral thing. Besides, it should be borne in mind that the spelling system changes very little over centuries, for being the normalized medium for pronunciation its stability is maintained by the literary and cultural standards that created it, and it consequently becomes, like Standard pronunciation, a general abstract norm that includes a majority of approximations. This is the spelling that survives in the accepted literature of a period, and by its very nature cannot afford the philologist the opportunity he needs. In dealing with the past he must, like Polonius, 'by indirections find directions out,' and so is forced to search for his material in such documents as have not on the whole preserved the educated spelling system, although it is well to remember that during the Early Modern period, when printing was in its infancy, the scribal tradition allowed a greater variation within the standard than we do nowadays, with the result that writers of a type who would not now depart from the norm frequently used personal phonetic spellings. These are especially valuable because indicative of the educated pronunciation of the period, but as time went on, and the literary standard became more closely bound up with printing, the spelling system tended to grow more and more precise, and occasional spellings of this nature consequently fewer.

Changes in pronunciation have been recorded, not so much within the educated system, as in colloquial deviations from it. The world has always had its poor spellers, who in their time are usually mocked at or at least amusedly tolerated—'we have a tedious ill spell'd letter from a dear sister,' says Edmund Verney's Oxford tutor in scorn—but it is they who after all perform for modern linguistic study the signal service of intimating in their 'occasional spellings' the pronunciation of their day. These spellings, as their name implies, are not necessarily mis- or bad spellings in the modern sense, for now most people have been trained to visualize words from print; they are rather improvisations on the part of those who, less under the influence of the literary standard, e.g. merchants, housewives,[1] messengers, etc., did not know the recognized symbols. They are for that reason invaluable to the student of language, and preponderate in this collection, but in interpreting them the young beginner should bear in mind one or two things concerning them, for their evaluation is attended by several difficulties. One cannot, for instance, argue from the Celys to Modern Received Standard, nor from the Verney ladies to B.B.C. pronunciation: area of origin must be given due weight. Again, individual spelling when unhampered by dictates of the standard is subject to many subtle influences; there is personal predilection for certain symbols, speech-consciousness (common in those unaccustomed to writing), imperfect phonetic analysis (still a common fault), interchangeability of symbols, tendencies to metathesis, varying values for the same symbol in different decades, and so on, all of which must be allowed for. And besides the vagaries or shortcomings of every writer it has to be remembered that in the majority of cases there is no absolute indication of vowel quantity, and a good deal of haziness in differentiation between monophthongs and diphthongs.[2] Any approach to the study of the occasional spelling must therefore be made with an alert mind. One of the surest guides to its value is its persistent recurrence in several documents over an extended period of time, for since the number of symbols in the spelling system is limited, identical, inverted, and other analogical spellings are very liable to be used by many writers to indicate the same

[1] Cf. also Swift's *Letter to a Young Lady*: 'It is a little hard, that not one gentleman's daughter in a thousand should be brought to read or understand her own natural tongue . . . and it is no wonder when they are not so much as taught to spell in their childhood, nor can ever attain to it in their whole lives.'

[2] See Ellis's *Early English Pronunciation*, vol. ii, especially pp. 118–60.

pronunciation; hence the larger the number of instances the philologist can gather, the better is he able to draw his inferences. The extracts in this collection are calculated to help the young student in this particular way; he will be able to multiply his examples, and by putting them in their correct setting with reference to authoritative grammars like Wyld's *Short History of English* and Jespersen's *Modern English Grammar*, will come to appreciate difficult sound-changes and developments that treated out of their context, as they must be in such complicated treatises, are sometimes apt to prove baffling. No examples are kept so well in mind as those one has sought for oneself, and to lighten the burden of the search has been one of my aims in making the compilation. The passages will not only provide matter for linguistic study, but also shed light on past customs and personalities. Diaries, letters, and journals have a perennial human interest, and one could not, I think, wish for a pleasanter way of learning historical grammar than by reading the naïve gossip of Harry Machyn, or the tender motherly letters of Lady Harley.

The following brief table of vowel and consonant changes has been appended as a guide; there is also an index to occasional spellings at the end of the book, to give the student a clue to the chain of evidence on which modern philological theory depends. I would advise him to read straight through the extracts first to gather a general impression of language development; afterwards he may study them in detail, both singly and in groups, e.g. all the extracts of one writer, those of a certain decade, of a certain area, etc.; or he may take each sound-change and trace its history through the centuries. By approaching the material from these several angles he will learn to place the sound-changes in their true perspective. C. D.

BANGOR, 1934.
B

EARLY NEW ENGLISH VOWEL AND CONSONANT CHANGES

TABLE OF PHONETIC SYMBOLS

VOWELS

ī as in *bee*

i ,, ,, *bit*

e ,, ,, *bet*

ę̄ long close e<ME. ę̣

ę̄ or ɛ̄ long open e<ME. ę̣.
   cf. *there* (ē is used to denote ME. letter and sound, [ɛ̄] to denote its phonetic value)

æ as in *bat*

ǣ æ lengthened

ā as in *father*

a as in first vowel of *bite*

ɔ̄ as in *saw*

ɔ ,, ,, *cot*

ǭ long close o<ME. ǫ̣. cf. first vowel sound in *boat*

ǭ long open o<ME. ǫ̣

ū as in *truth*

u ,, ,, *put*

ə̄ ,, ,, *turn*

ə ,, ,, *above*

ʌ ,, ,, *shut*

y ME. ẏ̆ and ü̆

CONSONANTS

p as in *pull*

b ,, ,, *but*

t ,, ,, *tap*

d ,, ,, *death*

k ,, ,, *cat*

g ,, ,, *go*

tʃ ,, ,, *church*

dʒ ,, ,, *judge*

m ,, ,, *man*

n ,, ,, *not*

ŋ ,, ,, *song*

l ,, ,, *lift*

ł ,, ,, *well*

f as in *fell*

v ,, ,, *velvet*

θ ,, ,, *thick*

ð ,, ,, *then*

s ,, ,, *silver*

z ,, ,, *zeal*

ʃ ,, ,, *shut*

ʒ ,, ,, *measure*

r ,, ,, *right*

h ,, ,, *help*

w ,, ,, *was*

 w̥ ,, ,, *which*

j ,, ,, *yet*

EARLY NEW ENGLISH VOWEL AND CONSONANT CHANGES

I. *The Stressed Vowels*

(a) *Short.*

ME. *a.*

> > fronted during fifteenth century to [æ]. Not generally accepted in educated speech until about the end of the sixteenth century. Spellings in. *e* indicate the change.
>
> *thetcher*, thatcher. *Settyrday*, Saturday. *Messe*, Mass.

ME. *a+l.*

> When not followed by another vowel, > [ɑul], the [ɑu] being later monophthongized to [ɔ]. Frequent spellings in *au, aw*, establish the diphthong early in the fifteenth century, but when monophthongization took place is not certain.[1]
>
> *aulmesse*, alms. *aull*, all. *fawlyn*, fallen.

ME. *ar+cons.*

> The *a* > [æ] as in the isolative development, but was subsequently lengthened before *r+cons.* to [ǣ], and later during the seventeenth century this lengthening was carried over to words in which *r* was not followed by a cons. The [ǣr] appears to have been retracted to [ɑ̄r] again, according to the spellings.
>
> *clarke*, clerk. *Clarkenwell*, Clerkenwell.

[1]See Wyld, *Short Hist.*, p. 191; Zachrisson, *Englische Studien*, vol. 53, pp. 313–14.

ME. *wa-*, *qua-*.

> When preceded initially by *w-* and *qu-*, *ă* > rounded to [o] or [ɔ]. The rounding appears to have begun early, but was not accepted in educated speech until well on in the seventeenth century.
>
> > *whos*, was.   *whot*, what.   *wosshyng*, washing. *quorill*, quarrel.

ME. *e*.

> Remained as [e], but before certain consonants, such as -*l*, -*ns*, etc., was frequently raised to [i].
>
> > *till*, tell.   *wilfar*, welfare.   *insinscible*, insensible.
>
> *e* < unrounded OE. *y* (Kent. *e*) and OF. *ü* occurs in Eastern and South-eastern texts.
>
> > *cherche*, church.   *Modbere*, Modbury.   *Bregys*, Bruges.
>
> For *geett*, *sleept*, where NE. has a shortened vowel, see ME. *ę̄*, p. 6.

ME. *er*.

> Either > *ar*, as above, or remained, in which latter case the vowel was lowered and flattened to [ɹ̄], with concurrent weakening of -*r*. Many words which now have [ɹ̄] developed according to the *ar*-type, and were especially common in the seventeenth and eighteenth centuries.
>
> > *hard*, heard.   *larne*, learn.   *marsy*, mercy.   *sarten*, certain.
>
> For *forn*, fern, see Index of Spellings.

ME. *i*.

> Appears to have remained as [i].   NE. *i*, however, is probably slacker.
>
> From the fifteenth to the eighteenth century spellings in -*e* are very frequent in all classes, which

points to a prevalent pronunciation with a lowered and slackened sound, perhaps [e].

beche, bitch. *bellowes,* billows. *chekons,* chickens, etc. It is worth noting in this connection that many speakers nowadays pronounce words like *pin, pen,* dangerously alike.

For *bushoppe, bosschope, buishop(es),* which represent a rounded [u] pronunciation, see Wyld, p. 159, n. 2.

ME. *i+r,* or *r+cons.*

In these combinations the vowel seems to have been early flattened, and made back, producing a sound similar to [ʌ]. Spellings in *u* indicate the change.

burth, birth. *furst, fust,* first.

With later weakening of *-r,* the vowel > lowered and lengthened to [ɔ]. Cf. the developments of *u, -ur, -er.*

ME. *o.*

This sound was probably like the German *o* in *Gott,* a mid-back-slack-round vowel, and appears to have remained until quite late in NE. It has now > lowered to [ɔ], but when this took place is uncertain.[1]

Unrounded *o,* indicated by spellings in *a,* was quite prevalent in polite speech until the eighteenth century; although it was (and is) also typical of West-country dialect, e.g.:

Trevelyan's *Tamsen,* Thompson (modern West Country, *Thomasine*).

For *Good, Gud,* God, which points to a long vowel, see Index of Spellings.

[1] See Ellis, *Early English Pronunciation,* i. 93-103.

ME. *o*+*s*, *f*, θ.

When followed by either of these spirants, *o* was lengthened and lowered to [ɔ]. Cf. such spellings as: *froath*, froth. *porsabell*, possible.

ME. *u*.

By the end of the seventeenth century had become fully unrounded to [ʌ]. The process probably began quite early (see Wyld, p. 184, for examples dating from 1469), but does not appear to have been thoroughly effected until the seventeenth century: this being the case, not only ME. *u*, but ENE. *u* < (i) ME. *ō*, and (ii) ME. *y* was also involved.

Indications of the old [u] pronunciation are common: *bwt*, but. *swche*, such. *goons*, guns.

But evidences of the new [ʌ] are much rarer. See next. For examples from other texts not quoted here, see Wyld, p. 184.

ME. *u*+*r*, or *r*+*cons*.

As in the case of *i* the vowel > [ʌ], and later with concurrent weakening of *r*, [ɔ].

Cf. *a* spellings like: *hart*, hurt. *wars*, worse (ME. *wurse*?). *charles*, churls.

ME. *ü* < OE. *y* and OF. *ü*.

> retracted to [u], thus falling together with ENE. [u] above, and was with it lowered and unrounded to [ʌ].

Dudcote, Didcot. *shurttes*, shirts, etc.

Regional forms in *e* (ME. *e*, OE. Kent. *y*) are frequent in early Eastern and South-eastern documents.

mess, *meche*, much. *sterrid*, stirred. *Modbere*, Modbury. *besinesse*, business, etc. See ME. *e*.

(b) *Long.*

ME. *ā.*

> Was early fronted and raised to [ɛ], and at this stage fell together with [ɛ] < ME. *ai, oi,* and *ę̄.* See pp. 6, 9, 10, 11.
>
> Hence inverse spellings like: *haith,* hath. *maid,* made. *laine,* lane.
>
> Later this [ɛ] was made tense [ę̄], and has now > diphthongized to [ei].
>
> See also the development of *ī.*

ME. *ā+r.*

> When followed by *-r,* ME. *ā* developed as above to [ɛ] and remained. With the weakening of *-r* a murmur vowel *ə* was developed, producing the combination [ɛ̄ə].
>
> *shayres,* shares. *shars,* shares.
>
> See *ę̄+r,* and *ai, ei+r.*

ME. *ę̄.*

> Was tensed to [ī]. Indications of the change are to be found in ME., and the frequency of *i* spellings in the fifteenth and sixteenth centuries goes to prove that the change was completely effected by the sixteenth. The development, however, seems to have varied considerably in different dialects. In some it was probably completed in the ME. period itself (see Wyld, p. 170).
>
> *dides,* deeds. *bisiche,* beseech. *kipe,* keep. *fry,* free. *wike,* week. *grives,* grieves.
>
> For *wake, woke,* week, see Index of Spellings.

ME. *ę̄+r.*

> The vowel developed to [ī] as above, and with

weakening of -*r*, and consequent development of
the murmur vowel *ə*, > combination [ī°].

hier, *hire*, hear, etc.

ME. *ę̄*.

Remained into the eighteenth century as [ɛ̄] or
[ẹ̄], but has now > tensed to [ī].

During the early modern period it fell together with
ME. *ā, ai*, and *ei*, as inverse spellings go to show:

hallthe, health. *eyse*, ease. *deyd*, dead, etc.

But what its exact quality was, [ɛ̄] or [ẹ̄], is uncertain.
It is probable that when ME. *ę̄* > [ī], ME. *ę̄* moved
to [ẹ̄].[1]

There are, however, some early evidences of the
existence of an [ī] pronunciation (see Wyld, p. 172),
and this latter gradually gained ground during the
seventeenth and eighteenth centuries, and has
finally > the accepted standard, with the exception
of a few words like *great, steak,* and *break*. These
were frequently pronounced [ī] in the eighteenth
century, as witness *grit*, great.

ME. *ę̄+r*.

Except in a group of words such as *beard, smear, ear,
spear*, etc., which have the tensed [ī], *ę̄* remained as [ɛ̄],
and with concurrent weakening of *r*, developed into the
combination [ɛ̄°]: but during the seventeenth and
eighteenth centuries, when *ę̄* was undergoing isolative
tensing, *ę̄+r* words were pronounced with [ɛ̄] and [ī].

Shortening of *ę̄*.

Many words which are now pronounced with short
[e] retained their original long vowel in the early
modern period. Spellings in *ee, ea*, are frequent.

geet, get. *sleept*, slept, etc.

[1] But see Wyld, pp. 171-3, and Jespersen, *Modern English
Grammar*, Part I, pp. 335-9.

ME. *i*.

Was diphthongized early in the fifteenth century to [ei], e.g:

heyff, hithe. *jeyst*, joist (OF. *giste*), etc.

But by about the end of the century the first element seems to have been flattened and retracted to a sound similar to [ə] or [ʌ], producing a diphthong identical with that developed from ME. *oi*. Inverted spellings in *oi*, *oy*, are fairly numerous.

voyne, vine. *asoynyd*, assigned.

This [ə] or [ʌ] has been subsequently slackened to [a], giving the NE. diphthong [ai], but, as in the case of the ME. ū below, there is a modern tendency towards monophthongization. Pronunciations in [ā], especially before -*r*, are fairly common in educated speech.

[fā], fire. [tāsʌm], tiresome, etc.

For *obleig*, etc., see Wyld, p. 187 n. 1.

ME. *ǭ*.

From the fourteenth century on this vowel underwent a gradual raising and rounding, but when the final [ū] stage was reached is uncertain. It must have been fairly early since many ME. *ǭ* words suffered shortening and fell together with ME. *ŭ*, and were unrounded with it to [ʌ]. See *u*.

Spellings in *oo*, *ou*, are common in early texts.

broother, brother. *bloud*, blood. *fforsouth*, forsooth, etc.

Spellings in *u* would seem to indicate early shortening to [u], but see Wyld, p. 177.

blud, blood. *fluddes*, floods, etc.

For *schoyn*, shoon, *noyne*, noon, see *oi*.

ME. ǭ+r.

The development is uncertain, some writers indicating the usual raising to [ū], others unrounding and lowering to [ɔ].

Spellings in *oor* point to [ūə]:

doorse, doors. *woorthy*, worthy (NE. [ə]).

ME. ǭ.

Until the sixteenth century appears to have remained, but the exact quality of the vowel is difficult to determine. It was probably a slack, round, mid-back vowel, similar to that heard in Welsh Regional Standard pronunciation of NE. ǭ words, [kǫt], coat; [bǫt], boat, etc., but since it seems to have fallen together for a time with the monophthongized form of *oi*, (see pp. 10–11), it may have been a little lower, and slightly more unrounded, approaching our present [ɔ]. See Jespersen, i. 92; iii. 531. It subsequently > tensed to [ọ], and finally diphthongized to NE. [ou]. Spellings in *oi*, *oy*, are quite common in South-eastern, Eastern, and London documents.

oith, oath. *alsoy*, also. *aloyne*, alone.

throughts, throats. (1642) may be an early instance of [ou].

For *won*, one, see Wyld, p. 179.

ME. ǭ+l.

During the fifteenth century an *u*-glide was developed before the back consonant *-l*, forming the combination [-oul].

behoulde, behold. *bould*, bold. *ould, howllde*, old, etc.

ME. ū (written *ou*).

Underwent early diphthongization, which has

resulted in NE. [au], although at present a monoph-thongized pronunciation [ā] is to be heard in edu-cated speech, e.g. [hɑs] house; [flɑs] flowers, etc. The early stages of the diphthongization are un-certain. According to the early grammarians *ū* first > [óu], or perhaps more correctly [ɔ́u], if spellings in *oy*, *o*, and *ou* are any indication.

   poyer, power. *oyer*, our. *hough*, how. *ore*, our, etc. Cf. the interesting *au* spellings cited by Zachrisson,[1] which seem to me to suggest a strong falling diph-thong, if not a monophthongal [ɔ].

II. *The Stressed Diphthongs*

ME. *ai, ei (ay, ey)*.

   ME. *ei* had already been levelled with ME. *ai* in the ME. period, and by the fifteenth century this [ɑi] had been levelled under the same sound as that developed from ME. *ā*; whether this was [ɛ̄] as mentioned above, p. 2, or the later [ei] is debatable.[2] Spellings in *e, a*, and occasionally *oi (oy)*, indicate the levelling.

   feth, faith. *nethor*, neither. *ordened*, ordained. *daly*, daily. *frad*, afraid. *invahar*, inveigher. *poynted*, painted, etc.

For *schynys*, chains, see Index of Spellings.

ME. *au*.

   By the sixteenth and seventeenth centuries appears

---

[1] Zachrisson (*English Pronunciation at Shakespeare's Time*, pp. 134–5), cites them as indicating [au], but as Wyld points out, it seems unlikely that they would be used to indicate this diphthong when the symbol was so commonly used for [ɔ]. My findings with regard to *oi* spellings for ME. *ū* seem to confirm the suggestion that they more probably indicate [ɔ̆ᵘ], or even [ɔ], before *-r*.

[2] See Jespersen, i. 323–8; Wyld, p. 194.

to have become monophthongized to a sound similar to [ɔ], through an [ou] or [ɔu] stage, when it was levelled under ME. *ou*. Early spellings in *ou* and *o* point to these changes.

chounge, 'chaunge,' change. *bycowse*, because. *cos*, cause.

And inverted spellings of *aw* for ME. *ou*. See below. Cf. also the *oy* spellings for ME. *ū*. ME. *-awn* words are commonly spelt *au*, *aw*.

aungels, angels. *nawnte* (aunt), but cf. *nowntes*, aunt's.

Eighteenth - century *aw* spellings are also fairly frequent.

ME. *oi, ui*.

The development of these diphthongs is exceedingly difficult to trace. According to the statements made by the grammarians, they seem to have been variously pronounced as diphthongs approximating to [oe],[1] [ui], or possibly a triphthong [oui], and [ɔi] in the fifteenth century; [oe], [ui], or [oui], [ɔi], and a new [ʌi], which fell together with the [ʌi], < ME. *ī*, in the sixteenth and seventeenth centuries, and [ɔi], [ʌi], and a few [ui] in the eighteenth. The occasional spellings on the whole confirm these pronunciations, *ai*, *ei*, and *ī* for *oi*, *ui*, and vice versa, being common.

vayage, voyage. *alay*, alloy. *peysaunt*, puissant. *Malweysy*, Malvoisie. *pyson*, poison. *implyed*, employed. *poynted*, painted. *aboye*, obey. *poyssaunt*, puissant. *powyssun*, poison. *owylle*, oil (?[oui]), etc.

But there are also a large number of spellings in
_____
[1] i.e. similar to [uᵉ]; see Ellis, op. cit., pp. 130–5.

o, ow, and *u* which strongly suggest that in spite of
the silence of the grammarians, there existed some
forms of monophthongal pronunciation as well.
It is possible that early in the modern period both
oi and *ui* were monophthongized to *ǭ* and *ū,*[1] and
that these pronunciations, common of course in
Scots, were characteristic also of Essex, and South-
eastern areas. They are found, however, in Oxon
and Bucks as late as the mid-eighteenth century.

By far the commonest spellings are *oi, oy* for ME. *ǭ.*

  oith, oythe, oath. *boyth,* both. *alsoy,* also, etc.

These are supported by *o* spellings for *oi.*

  closter, cloister. *posynners,* poisoners. *assole,*
  assoil. *disaponted,* disappointed. *voces,* voices, etc.

And further by *oy* spellings for ME. *ou,* and inversely
ou, ow spellings for *oi.*

  poyer, power. *oyer,* our. *boythe, both,* bought, etc.
  owle, oil. *clowster,* cloister. *disapounted,* disappointed. *disloualty,* disloyalty, etc.

  See *ou.*

ME. *ou.*

By slackening and lowering of the first element
> a slow falling diphthong [ɔu], and with subsequent
weakening of the second was monophthongized and
lengthened to [ɔ̄]. As has been noted above, it
fell together with ME. *au* and *oi (ui)* during its
development. For the coalescence of *ǭ* and *ou* in
the seventeenth–eighteenth centuries see Jespersen,
i. 326; ii. 36 ff.

  thawgh, though. *boythe, both,* bought, etc.

ME. *eu, iu, ǖ.*

Have all now > either [ju] or [ū], but the develop-

[1] See. Luick, *Historische Grammatik der englischen Sprache,* p.
481 n. 2., and Zachrisson, op. cit., p. 65.

ment is very uncertain. See Wyld, p. 193. It seems that all three sounds were early—about the fifteenth century — levelled under one sound, approximating to [jü], which was retained by some speakers, and retracted to [ju] by others, and later in many words, especially after *r* and *l*, this [ju] > [ū]. Spellings in *y, ew, eu, u, ue, uw, we*, etc., occur for words of all origins, and point to the levelling in pronunciation.

> *comyned*, communed. *contenew*, continue. *deukes*, dukes. *surte*, surety. *crue*, crew. *druw*, drew. *knwe*, knew, etc.

III. *The Unstressed Vowels and Diphthongs*

During the ENE period all vowels and diphthongs in unaccented syllables, whether initial, medial, or final, were considerably weakened. As a rule the front vowels, including [æ] < original *a* tended to be further fronted to [i]; back-rounded vowels were unrounded and reduced to an indistinct sound similar to [ʌ] or [ə]; and the diphthongs were monophthongized, *oi* becoming [i], *ai, ei* [e], later [i], and *au, ou,* [ʌ] and [ə], although in some cases these last were fronted to [e] and [i]. No hard and fast rules can be laid down, for analysis of unaccented sounds is so delicate that to the ordinary man's ear there seems little difference between one and another; hence the indecisions in spelling so common in the fifteenth and sixteenth centuries, e.g. *banurs, banars, baners*, banners; *compeny, cumpony, compyny*, company, etc.

The following examples may serve as a guide:

a.   *perticuller*, particular. *embassador, imbassador,* ambassador. *carictor*, character. *marigh*, marriage.

Donkister, Doncaster. *messinger*, messenger (ME. *messager*). *Mykaellmes*, Michaelmas. *perticuller*, particular.

e. *imbraced*, embraced. *intertained*, entertained. *ironyos*, erroneous. *enimyes*, enemies. *satesfy*, satisfy. *libarty*, liberty. *thankyth*, thanketh. *Estyr*, Easter. *offisirs*, officers. *rasis*, races. *linin*, linen. *remembre*, remember. *minestar*, minister. *aparant*, apparent.

i. *minestar*, minister. *confedent*, confident. *medeson*, medicine. *posable*, *porsabell*, possible. *marques*, marquis.

o. *abedyensses*, obediences. *pressessyon*, procession. *prisenor*, prisoner. *sesyn*, season. *harlettes*, harlots. *bysschyp*, bishop.

u. *apon*, upon. *Settyrday*, *Saterday*, Saturday. *sulfer*, sulphur.

ü. *prediditiall*, prejudicial. *venter*, *ventaros*, venture, venturous. *pleshar*, *plesshur*, pleasure. *departor*, departure. *misfortin*, misfortune.

ai, ei. *Sent*, *Sant*, Saint. *sarten*, certain. *travell*, travail. *bargenyng*, bargaining. *chaplyne*, chaplain. *curtese*, courtesy (ME. *curteisie*). *the*, they (in unstressed positions).

au, ou. *ffeolaship*, fellowship.

IV. *The Consonants*

The occasional spelling is particularly valuable in indicating consonant change, for, as a rule, consonant symbols tend to be used more easily and correctly than vowel symbols by all classes of speakers. During the early Modern period natural tendencies to add, drop, assimilate, coalesce, and change sounds were not restricted in educated

c

speech, with the result that what we should now be inclined to consider provincial or even vulgar pronunciation, e.g. *ruing*, ruin; *walkin*, walking; *hable*, able; *thousant*, thousand; *hosbon*, husband, etc., was then accepted in all forms of polite speech, and continued to be characteristic of the language until well on in the eighteenth century. Since then, however, an artificial standard of 'correctness' has been fostered, largely by academic influences; the printed word has been made the criterion for pronunciation, and the majority of these older, natural changes have given place to more meticulous and rigid pronunciations.

The more important changes which occurred during the period from the fifteenth to the eighteenth century are given below in a general but convenient classification.

(a) *Addition*.

  (i) [j], written *y*, was frequently developed initially before front vowels.

> *yeven*, even. *yerly*, early. *yel*, ill, etc.

  Characteristic of all areas until the mid-eighteenth century.

  (ii) Parasitic consonants were developed finally, more especially after liquids, nasals, and the two spirants, *s* and *f*.

> *puld*, pull. *Newe Castelle uppon Tynde*, Newcastle-on-Tyne.

  (iii) Initial vowels in stressed positions were often aspirated.

> *Hane*, Ann. *hale*, ale. *hable*, able, etc.

(b) *Loss*.

  (i) (*g*)*h* was lost initially and before -*t*.

> *alff*, half. *affe*, have. *ould*, hold, etc. *fitt*, fight. *weythe*, weight. Inversely *ought*, out, etc.

(ii) *l* was usually dropped before lip-consonants.

> *behaf*, behalf. *genttywoman*, gentilwoman. *wod*, would, etc.

But the *l* in *would*, *should*, and *could* (where it is analogical, ME. *coude*) was pronounced in stressed positions until the seventeenth century.

> *whollde*, *whowlde*, *woold*. *sshuwlde*, *coould*, etc.

(iii) *d* and *t* were either assimilated or lost before an immediate following consonant, and dropped when final.

> *Wensday*, Wednesday. *hanfull*, handful. *granmothar*, grandmother. *respecks*, respects. *hosbon*, husband. *thousens*, thousands. *worll*, world. *patton*, patent, etc.

(iv) *b* was sometimes lost medially before another consonant, and finally.

> *nimlest*, nimblest. *humely*, humbly.

(v) *f* (*ph*) sometimes lost when final.

> *Asse*, Asaph. *Randol*, Randolph.

(vi) *r* was early lost before consonants, especially *s*.

> *fudermore*, furthermore. *fust*, first. *foster*, forester.

(vii) *w* was lost (i) in initial syllables before a back round vowel, and (ii) in unstressed positions.

> *sor*, swore. *tordis*, towards.

(viii) *v* was lost when intervocalic, and between a vowel and a consonant.

> *marlys*, marvels. *Candish*, Cavendish.

(c) *Voicing and Unvoicing.*

(i) Stops were both voiced and unvoiced initially,

medially when intervocalic, and between a vowel and a consonant, and finally.

bay, pay. *Blages*, Blake's. *debety*, deputy. *sugess*, success. *servand*, servant, etc. *senkyll*, single. *Hearifort*, Hereford. *thousant*, thousand. *sende*, sent, etc.

Cf. also the interchange between [tʃ] and [dʒ] in: *dydge*, ditch. *discharchyng*, discharging.

(ii) *wh* initially > voiced to [w̥].

Cf. inverse spellings like:

whos, was. *whe*, we. *whor*, were, etc.

(d) *Isolative changes.*

(i) ME. -(g)h, -(g)ht when final > [f], [ft].

daftere, daughter. *frayfte*, freight. *ybofte*, bought. *unsoffethe*, unsought.

In -(g)ht words this f pronunciation, which appears to have lasted into the eighteenth century, has now > obsolete in educated speech, except in the case of *laughter*.

(ii) *f* and *v* > interchangeable with [θ] and [ð]. See Jespersen, i. 13·9.

heyff, hithe. *Meredifes*, Meredith's. *havef*, haveth. *livef*, liveth, etc.

(iii) *w* and *v* > interchangeable.

wellffete, velvet. *wochesaf*, vouchsafe. *awise*, avise. *Dowyr*, Dover. *Medevey*, Medway.

(iv) *t* and *th* > interchangeable, especially in the neighbourhood of *r*.

thechyng, teaching. *Garthere*, Garter. *comfforth*, comfort. *douth*, doubt. *Bartylmew*, Bartholemew.

(v) *d* and *t* and *th* > interchangeable.
> *do*, to. *ther*, dare. *þepartyd*, departed. *laboryd*,
> laboureth. *Mondeforth*, Moundford, etc.
> See Jespersen, i. 208 ff.

(vi) Initial, medial, and final *s* and *ts*, frequently >
[ʃ] and [tʃ].
> *shoulders*, soldiers. *schynys*, chains. *schardyge*,
> charge. *shamba*, chamber. *Porchemouth*, Ports-
> mouth. *toshith*, toucheth. *prynche*, prince, etc.

Spellings in *ss* often indicate [ʃ]. Cf.:
> *pleasse*, please. *pesse*, piece. *powyssun*, poison;
> beside inverse spellings like *flesse*, flesh. *popysse*,
> popish. *fassioned*, fashioned, etc.

(vii) Initial *wh* > *h* (or *w* is lost?).
> *hole*, whole. *hos*, whose. *hensse*, whence. *hurlpole*,
> whirlpool, etc.

(viii) *n* is substituted for [ŋ] in unaccented syllables.
Very common in the seventeenth and eighteenth
centuries.
> *Abendon*, Abingdon. *bein*, being. *lodgens*, lodgings.
> *walkin*, walking. Cf. *amonst*, amongst.

(ix) *u* > *v, f* in the word *lieftenantes*, lieutenants.
See Jespersen, i. 10·28.

(e) *Combinative changes.*
(i) Initial *su*, [sjü or sjū] > [ʃū]. This change is often
indicated by spellings in *sh*.
> *asshureanc*, assurance.

(ii) Medial *su*, [ʒj] > [ʒ]. This change is also indicated
by spellings in *sh*, but it is uncertain whether the
sound was always voiced.
> *plesshur, pleshar*, pleasure.

(iii) Medial *-si-*, *-ti-*, [sj, tj] > [ʃ].
   reselushons, resolutions.

(iv) Medial *-di-*, *-du-*, [dj, dju] > [dʒ, dʒū].
   sogers, soldiers, as beside *soudeours* (ME. *souldier*, *soudeour*, *sougeor*).

For detailed history of consonant changes see Jespersen, vol. i, and Wyld, chap. viii.

ILLUSTRATIVE EXTRACTS

CHRONOLOGICAL LIST OF SOURCES

1420–42. *The Letters of Queen Margaret of Anjou, and Bishop Beckington.* (Camden Soc.)

1440–70. *The Paston Letters.* (Ed. Gairdner.)

1447–50. *The Shillingford Papers.* (Camden Soc.)

1451–2. *The Chronicle of William Gregory, in Historical Collections of a Citizen of London.* (Camden Soc.)

[1290]–1483. *The Stonor Letters and Papers.* (Camden Soc.)

1470. *Warkworth's Chronicle.* (Camden Soc.)

1471. *Historie of the Arrival of King Edward IV.* (Camden Soc.)

1477. William Caxton's *History of the Life of Jason.* (E.E.T.S.)

1473–88. *The Cely Papers.* (Camden Soc.)

1482. *The Revelation to the Monk of Evesham.* (Arber's Reprints.)

1482. *The Archives of the Corporation of the City of London.* (Letter Bk. L, folios 182–184b.)

*c.*1494–1556. *The Greyfriars Chronicle, London.* (Camden Soc.)

1503–4. Sir Henry Ellis, *Original Letters Illustrative of English History.* 3 vols.

1504–1776. *The Trevelyan Papers,* vol. iii. (Camden Soc.)

1517–18. *The Pilgrimage of Sir Richard Torkington.* (Ed. W. J. Loftie.)

1531. Sir Thomas Elyot's *The Booke Named the Gouernour.*

1550–63. *The Diary of Henry Machyn.* (Camden Soc.)

1555–8. *The Life of Bishop Fisher.* (E.E.T.S.)

1572–88. *The Bardon Papers.* (Camden Soc.)

1579. Stephen Gosson's *Schoole of Abuse.* (Arber's Reprints.)

1581–93. *Dr. Dee's Diary.* (Camden Soc.)

[1572]–1602. *The Letters of Queen Elizabeth and James VI.* (Camden Soc.)

[1580]–1622. *The Stiffkey Papers.* (Camden Soc.)

1625–43. *The Letters of Lady Brilliana Harley.* (Camden Soc.)

1639–96. *Memoirs of the Verney Family.* 4 vols. (Ed. Lady Verney. Longmans, Green & Co.)

1644. *Ralph Josselin's Diary.* (Camden Soc.)

1656. *The Autobiography of Ann, Lady Halkett.* (Camden Soc.)

[1687]–1700. *Correspondence of the Family of Hatton.* (Camden Soc.)

1705–39. *The Wentworth Papers.* (Ed. J. J. Cartwright. 1883.)

ILLUSTRATIVE EXTRACTS

From RICHARD BOKELAND, Treasurer of Calais,

To a friend or brother

1428.

Right worshipfull Brother, I commende me to yow, etc.

. . . there as my lordes letters maketh mencion, that
I shulde gouvern me as tenderly as I can in preferring the
payments due to my saide lorde of Warrewyk, God knoweth
my will were to plese my lord of Warrewyk in that or in
any other thing to me possible; but it is harde for me to
preferre thos payments withouten importable maugre [1] on
other parties. Considering that all thassignements of
Caleys wol noȝt suffice yerely to paye my lorde [2] and his
soudeours and the remenant of the Cappitaines of the
Marches, that is to saye, my lord of Gloucestre and his
souldeours of theire part, and semblably other captaines of
theires, so that the preferment of my saide lorde of Warrewyk moste of necessite cause my lorde and his souldeours
to renne [3] much the more in dette, the whiche I mooste
charge. Natheles, yf my lorde wol algates [4] that it so be,
I pray yow certify me thereof and I shall be redy til [5] obeye
his commandement with right good wille as my dutee
requireth yn that and in all other to my powaire, while I
leve,[6] with Gods grace, that ever have yow in his hooly
keping and grante yow right goode lyf and longe. . . .

The Letters of Queen Margaret of Anjou, etc.

[1] Unbearable ill-will or disadvantage.   [2] The Duke of Bedford.
     [3] Run.   [4] In any case.   [5] To.   [6] Live.

23

From Bishop Beckington,[1]

  To Master John Somerset

London.   *June 1442.*

My right welbeloved and entierly trusted Maister,

 After due recommendacion, beying nowe in the utter-most parties of this world,[2] and abidyng my M[aster] Roos, which, as I suppose, is taried for the dawngrous tydyings that my M[aster] Hull hath reported unto the Kinge, which, as I suppose ben not unknowyn unto yow, touching the greet jepart [3] in passyng unto the countrey that we be sent unto, beseching youe, consideryng the matier that we be sent forth fore, which shulde be not or litell fructueux, as in my conceyt, withoute hasty remedy be hadde in that behaf, ye wol sture [4] and call upon my lords of the Kings Counsaill, to pourvey such remedye in this partie,[5] in all goodely hast, as yt maye be to the Kings pleasure, and the wele of us all; and that ye wol, in the most humble wise, recommende me unto the Kings moost high and noble grace, etc.

        Yor chappelleyn,

           T. B.

      The Letters of Bishop Beckington.

From Margaret Paston,

   To her husband, John Paston

Norfolk.   *28th Sept.* 1443.

 Ryth worchipful hosbon, I recomande me to yow, desyryng hertely to her of yowr wilfar, thanckyng God of yowr a mendyng of the grete dysese that ye have hade, and

---

[1] Bishop of Bath and Wells and secretary to Henry VI.   [2] Exeter.
    [3] Jeopardy.   [4] Stir.   [5] Part.

I thancke yow for the letter that ye sent me, for be my trowthe my moder and I wer nowth in hertys es fro the tyme that we woste of yowr sekenesse, tyl we woste verely of your a mendyng. My moder be hestyd [1] a nodyr ymmage of wax of the weytte of yow to oyer [2] Lady of Walsyngham, and sche sent iiij nobelys to the iiij Orderys of Frerys at Norweche to pray for yow, and I have be hestyd to gon on pylgreymmays [3] to Walsingham, and to Sent Levenardys [4] for yow; be my trowth I had never so hevy a sesyn as I had from the tyme that I woste of yowr sekenesse tyl I woste of yowr a mendyng, and ȝyth [5] myn hert is in no grete esse, ne nowthe xal be, tyl I wott that ȝe ben very hal. . . .

I pray yow hertely that [ye] wol wochesaf to sende me a letter as hastely as ȝe may, yf wry[t]yn [6] be non dysesse to yow, and that ye wollen wochesaf to sende me worde quowe [7] your sor dott.[8] Yf I mythe have had my wylle, I xulde a seyne yow er dystyme; I wolde ye wern at hom . . . lever dan a goune, ȝow [9] it wer of scarlette.[10] . . .

Yorys,

M. PASTON.

The Paston Letters:

From JOHN SHILLINGFORD, Mayor of Exeter,

To his Corporation

Exeter.   *2nd Nov.* 1447.

Worthy Sires, as yn the other letter, etc., y grete yow well alle. Yn the whiche letter y wrote to yow that y

---

[1] Promised, vowed.   [2] Our.   [3] Pilgrimage.   [4] St. Leonard's (Priory, Norwich).   [5] Yet, still.   [6] Writing.   [7] How.   [8] Doth (does).   [9] Though. Margaret had been promised a new frock.   [10] One of the finest and most expensive medieval cloths.

hadde a dey to appere before the lordis for oure mater [1] the Fridey next ther after; and for as moche as my lord Chaunceller bade the Justyse to dyner ayenst that same day for oure mater, seyyng that he sholde have a dys [2] of salt fisshe; y hiryng [3] this, y didde as me thoght aughte to be done, and by avys of the Justise and of oure counseill, and sende [4] thider that day ij stately pikerellis [5] and ij stately tenchis, for the whiche my lord Chaunceller cowde [6] right grete thankys and made right moche therof hardely.[7] . . .

The morun tuysday al Halwyn yeven,[8] y receyved the answeris to oure articulis at Westminster, of the whiche y sende yow a true copy, yn the whiche articulis as hit appereth they have spatte out the uttmyst and worste venym that they cowde seye or thynke by me . . . but as for trawthe of the mater that tocheth me, meny worthy man stondeth on the same cas, and have do [9] moche werce than ever y didde . . . therfor y take right noght by,[10] . . . and am right mery and fare right well, ever thankyng God and myn awne purse. And y liyng on my bedde atte writyng of this right yerly,[11] myryly syngyng a myry song, and that ys this, *Come no more at oure hous, come, come, come.* Y woll not dye nor for sorowe ne for anger . . . while y have mony, but that ys and like to be scarce with me, considerynge the bisynesse and coste that y have hadde. . . . Y can no more attis [12] tyme, but y pray you to be not

[1] A quarrel between the Mayor and Bishop of Exeter concerning their respective rights of jurisdiction: the mayor claimed it over whole city, including the bishop's palace; the bishop claimed that he held the see separate from the city.

[2] Dish.　　　[3] Hearing.　　　[4] Sent.　　　[5] Pickerels, pike.

[6] Expressed, offered; see O.E.D. s.v. *Can*, iii. 10.

[7] Heartily, profusely.　　　[8] All Hallows' Eve, i.e. 31st October.

[9] Done.　　　[10] I care nothing for it.　　　[11] Early.　　　[12] At this

wery to over rede, hire and se all the writyng that y have
sende home to you . . . and God be with yow.

The Shillingford Papers.

From QUEEN MARGARET (of Anjou), wife of Henry VI,
  To THE MASTER OF ST. GILES'S HOSPITAL [1]
London.   *c.* 1447.

By the Queene.

Trusty, etc., and for asmoche as we be enfourmed that
oon Robert Uphome, of the age of xvii yere, late querester [2]
unto the moost reverende fader in God our beal uncle [3] the
cardinal, whom God assoile, atte his college at Winchestre,
is now by Godds visitacion become lepour; we desire
therfore and praye you, sith he hath noon other socour ne
lyvelode to lyve upon but oonly of aulmesse of cristen
peuple as it is saide, that at reverence of our blessed
Creatour and in contemplacion of this o[r] prayer, ye will
accepte and receive hym into yo[r] hospital of Seint Giles,
unto such findinge and lyvelode as other personnes ther in
suche cas be accustomed to have, as we trust you.   In
which thinge, ye shul not oonly do a right meritorie dede to
Godds pleasir but deserve also of us right especial thanke,etc.

The Letters of Queen Margaret of Anjou.

From QUEEN MARGARET (of Anjou), wife of Henry VI,
  To SIR JOHN FORESTER
London   *c.* 1447.

By the Queene.

Trusty and welbeloved,—We late yow wite,[4] that this

---

[1] St. Giles of the Lepers, a hospital for lepers founded in 1117,
by Maud, Queen of Henry I; it contained room for forty lepers, to
whose upkeep the queen contributed sixty shillings a year for
each inmate.

[2] Chorister.   [3] Uncle-in-law.   [4] We give you to understand.

same day ther have be bifore us a greete multitude both of men and women, our tenants of oure lordship of Herting-fordbury,[1] compleyning them that ye have, and yet be dayly about to destroie and undo them for ever; in so fer[th] forth that ye have do many of them to be wrongfully endited nowe late of felonye before the crowner, by yo[r] owne familier servantes and adherents, not knowyng the trouth of the mater; and many of theym ye do kepe in prisonne, and the remenant of oure tenants dar not abide in theire houses for fer of deth and other injuries that ye dayly do them; and al by colour of a ferme that ye have there of oures that, as it is said, for yo[r] owne singler lucre [2] ye wrongfully engrose towards you al oure tenants lyvelode there; not ownly unto grete hindering and undowyng of oure said tenants, and also unto grete derogacion and prejudice of us and of oure said lordship; wherof we mervel greetly; and in especial that ye that be jugge [3] wold take so parceably [4] the wrongfull destruccion of oure said tenants. Wherfore we wol, and expressly exhorte and require yow, that ye leve yo[r] said labors and besinesse, in especial ayeinst us and oure said tenants, until tyme that ye have communed and declared you in this mater before us; and that, the meene while, ye do suffre oure tenants that be in prisonne to be mainprissed [5] under sufficient seurtie; and the remenant of oure tenants giltlesse that be fled for fere of yo[r] destruccion may come home unto oure said lordship. And if eny of oure tenants have offended ayeinst the laws, oure entent is that the trouth knowen, he shalbe peynfully punysshed, and chastised as the cas requireth. And howe ye thinke to be disposed therin ye will aserteine us, by the bringer of thise, wherto we shall truste; as ye desire to

---

[1] In Herts.   [2] Private profit.   [3] Judge.
[4] Peaceably.   [5] Released.

stande in the tendre and faverable remembrance of oure grace therfor, in tyme comyng.   Yeven, etc., at Wynds[or].

The Letters of Queen Margaret of Anjou.

From JOHN SHILLINGFORD, Mayor of Exeter,

To RICHARD DRUELL [1]

Exeter.   *Lent* 1447/8.

Furst ye shall recommende the Maier and all the hole comminalte of the Cite of Excetre to my lorde Chaunceller is gode and gracyous lordship of his awne puple and true bedmen,[2] and at his commaundement at alle tyme redy, and that this be seide with more, after your discrecyon yn the most godely wyse and under the most best and convenyent termys as longeth to his high astate and plesure as lord. . . .

Item, ye shall enfourme my lorde how . . . Sir Rogger Kys, chanon [3] . . . wolde no ferther yn that [mater], but moved and stured [4] of other divers entreteys.[5]   And y seide ayen, sithen that they wolde leye this entrety apart, what ever entrety they wolde move, sture or desire resonable, hit sholde be aggreed, so that no defaute shoulde be founde yn oure part; wherapon we comyned [6] of divers maters and entretyes, and atte last we conducended [7] yn this wyse; ij men to be nempted [8] of ayther counseyll to sette ayther party yn rule of entrety . . . [and how . . .]

___

[1] One of the councillors, and member of the corporation.

[2] Beadsmen. Lit., those paid to pray for others: here, true friends, subjects.

[3] Canon of Exeter Cathedral.   [4] Stirred.   [5] Negotiations, terms.

[6] Communed, discussed.   [7] Came to agreement, decided.

[8] Named.

D

The morun at viii atte cloke came to the Mayer my lorde
of Exceter is surveyour . . . and warned hym that my
seyde lord Bysshop of Exceter wolde be att Exeter that
same dey atte oon atte clokke to speke with hym. . . .
Among other next aboveseide my seide lorde [1] commaunded
the seide Maier to shewe that speciall writyng that he hadde
promysed to my lorde Chaunceller that sholde make an
ende of all the mater, and ther apon he stiked fast with
stroynge [2] longage and chere, as well as yn other maters
aboveseide.

The Shillingford Papers.

From JOHN SHILLINGFORD, Mayor of Exeter,

To his deputy in London

Exeter.   *Easter* 1448.

Ferthermore, y pray yow what reporte that ever hath
be made ayenst us by the Chanons part afore this tyme,
for oure blame, that noght withstondynge, that ye reporte
the beste and as trewthe is of theyre gode and sad [3] govern-
aunce sithen oure departynge fro London, for theire thanke
and worship; [4] ffor, by my trawthe, they and alle theyris
by theyre governance have governed ham yn the most
best, gentyll and saddist wise, to all ententis sithen oure
departynge fro London.   Ferst, they, seynge [5] the streyte
rule that the Mayer sette in the Cite for kepynge of the pees,
they confourmed ham to the same, and ruled ham and alle

---

[1] i.e. the bishop, when he met Shillingford.
[2] Strong, firm, or (?) strange.   [3] Earnest.
[4] In thanks and honour to them.   [5] Seeing.

theyris ther after,[1] and so, blessed be God, that all nyght-walkynge, yvell longage, visagynge,[2] sholdrynge,[3] and all riatous rule is lefte. . . . God continue hit! For y ther [4] seye hit feithfully, yf this rule had be [5] had and kept a fore this tyme, we hadde never be yn this debate. . . . And thus hit semeth that longe tarynge of delyverynge of the articulis . . . hath do eyse,[6] pryvynge [7] the wyll and the pacyence of bothe parties; . . . with this, [pray] that my saide Lord Chaunceller be gode and gracious Lorde to oure partie to have resonable dey to make an answere to the articulis, considerynge longe tyme that they have hadde yn makynge of the articulis, fro the xv^e of Seynt Hillary yn to the xv^e of Pasche; and yet they have not nywe made ham, but corrected the olde, that were delyvered to us yn the xv^e of Seynt Mighell,[8] yn the whiche the substance of the nywe articulis ys myche comprehended. . . .

And y pray yow, what was seyde yn the Gildehall at Excetre a Trusday [9] yn the Ester wyke,[10] first of oure Soverayne Lorde the Kynge, afterwarde of my Lorde Chaunceller, and how the puple beth willed and set, foryete [11] ye hit noght.

The Shillingford Papers.

From MARGARET PASTON,
     To her husband, JOHN PASTON
Norfolk.   *April* 1448.

. . . [12] Than I prayd her aȝyn that sche wuld teryn [13] tyl ȝe kom hom, and I seyd I trostyd veryly that ȝe wuld don

---

[1] According to it (i.e. the rule).   [2] Grimacing.   [3] Jostling.
[4] Dare.   [5] Been.   [6] Ease.   [7] Proving, testing.   [8] St. Michael.
[9] On Thursday.   [10] Week.   [11] Forget.
[12] Lady Morley was demanding payment of a certain relief from John Paston.   [13] Tarry.

qhan ӡe kom hom, as itt longeth to ӡw to don; and if ӡe myth have very knowleche that sche awyth [1] of ryth for to have itt, I seyd I wyst wel that ӡe wuld pay it with ryth gode wyl, and told her that ӡe had sergyd [2] to a fownd wrytyng therof, and ӡe kwd non fynd in non wyse. And sche sayd sche wyst wele there was wrytyng therof inow, and sche hath wrytyng therof hw Syr Robert of Mawthby, and Sir Jon, and my grawnsyre, and dyverse other of myn awncesterys payd it, and seyd nevyre nay therto. And in no wyse I kwd not geyn no grawnth of her to sesyn [3] tyl ӡe kom hom. . . .

Laueraw[n]ce Rede of Mawth[b]y recommawndeth hym to ӡu, and prayt ӡw that ӡe wyl vwchesave to leten hym byn [4] of ӡw the ferm barly that ӡe xuld have of hym, and if ӡe wyl laten hym have it to a resonably pris, he wyl have it with ryth a gode wyl; and he prayit ӡw if ӡe wyl that he have it, that ӡe wyl owche save [5] to send hym word. . . .

The Holy Trynyte have ӡw in hys kepyng, and send ӡw helth and gode spede in all ӡour maters twchyng ӡour ryth.

Wretyn at Norwyche, on the Wedenys day nexst after thatt ӡe partyd hens.

Yors,

Margarete Paston.

The Paston Letters.

From Queen Margaret (of Anjou), wife of Henry VI,
To the Keeper of Abchild Park

London.   28*th August* 1449.

By the Queene.

Welbeloved, we wol and expressly charge you that, for certein consideracions moving us, our game within our parc

---

[1] Ought.   [2] Searched.   [3] Cease.   [4] Buy.   [5] Vouchsafe.

of Apechild,[1] wherof ye have the sauf garde and keping, ye do, with all diligence, to be cheresshed, favered and kept without suffryng eny personne of what degre, estat or condicion that he be, to hunte there, or have course, shet,[2] or other disporte, in amentising [3] oure game above said, to thentent that, at what tyme it shall please us to resorte thedre, yo[r] trew acquital may be founden for the good keping and replenishing therof, to thaccomplissement of o[r] entencion in this partie. And that in no wise ye obeie ne serve eny other warrant, but if hit be under our signet, and signed with o[r] owne hande. And if eny personne presume tattempte to the contrarie of the premisses, ye do certiffie us of their names; and that he faill not herof, as ye will eschew our displeasure, at yo[r] perill, and upon forfaiture of the kepyng of o[r] said park. Yeven, etc., at Plasshe,[4] the xxviii day of Auguste, the yere etc.

The Letters of Queen Margaret of Anjou, etc.

From William Gregory's [5] *Chronicle*

London. *c.* 1451-2.

1450. And that Phylyppe Malpas [6] was aldyrman, and they spoylyd hym ande bare away moche goode of hys, and in specyalle moche mony, bothe of sylvyr and golde, the valowe of a notabylle som, and in specyalle of marchaundys, as of tynne, woode, madyr [7] and alym [8] . . . and many a ryche clothe of arys,[9] to the valewe of a notabylle sym— *nescio, set* [10] *Deus omnia scit.* Ande in the evenynge they

---

[1] Abchild, near Great Waltham, Essex. [2] Shooting.
[3] ? Improving, protecting. [4] Pleshy, a few miles from Abchild.
[5] Wm. Gregory, Mayor of London, 1451-2: a skinner by trade.
[6] Robbed by Jack Cade's rebels. [7] Madder, for dyes. [8] Alum.
[9] Arras. [10] *Sed.*

went whythe hyr sympylle captayne to hys loggynge; botte
a certayne [1] of hys sympylle and rude mayny a bode there
alle the nyght, wenyge [2] to them that they hadde wytte and
wysdome for to have gydyde or put in gydyng all Ingelonde,
alsosone a[s] they hadde gote the cytte of London by a
mysse happe of cuttynge of ij sory cordys [3] that nowe be
alteryde, and made ij stronge schynys [4] of yryn unto the
draught brygge of London. But they hadde othyr men
with hem, as welle of London as of there owne party.
And by hem of on parte, and of that othyr parte they lefte
noo thyng unsoffethe,[5] and they serchyd alle that nyght. . . .

And uppon the xij day of Juylle, the yere a fore sayde,
the sayde camptayne was cryde and proclaymyd traytoure,
by the name of John Cade, in dyvers placys of London,
and also in Sowtheworke, whythe many moo, that what
man myght or wolde bryng the sayde John Cade to the
kyng, qwyke or dede, shulde have of the kynge a thousande
marke.

From William Gregory's *Chronicle* [6]

London.   *c.* 1451–2.

1429. And my Lorde of Warwyke bare the kynge to
chyrche in a clothe of scharlet furryd, . . . And thenne
he was led up in to the hyghe schaffold, whyche schaffolde
was coveryd alle with saye [7] by twyne the hyghe auter and
the quere. And there the kyng was sette in hys sete in
the myddys of the schaffold there, beholdynge the pepylle
alle aboute saddely and wysely. . . . Thenne the kynge

---

[1] A certain number.   [2] Weening.
[3] Jack Cade had entered London by cutting the two cords of the
draw-bridge.   [4] Chains.   [5] Unsought.
[6] From the description of Henry VI's coronation.   [7] Silk.

went unto the hyghe auter, and humely layde hym downe
prostrate, hys hedde to the auter warde, longe tyme lyyng
stylle. Thenne the arche byschoppys and byschoppys
stode rounde a boute hym, and radde exercysyons [1] ovyr
hym, and many antemys i-song by note. And thenne the
arche byschoppes wente to hym and strypte hym owte of
hys clothys in to hys schyrte. And there was yn hys
schyrte a thynge lyke grene taffata, whyche was i-lasyd
at iiij placys of hym. Thenne was he layde downe a yenne
and helyd [2] hym with hys owne clothys yn the same manner
a fore sayde. And thenne the Byschoppe of Chester, and
of Rouchester songe a letany ovyr hym. And the Arche-
byschoppe of Cantyrbury radde many colettys [3] ovyr hym.
Thenne the archebyschoppys toke hym uppe a gayne and
unlasyd hym, and a noyntyd hym . . . and on hys hedde
they putt on a whyte coyffe of sylke. And so he wentte
viij dayes; and at the viij dayes the byschoppys dyde wasche
hit a waye with whyte wyne i-warmyd leuke warme. . . .

From William Gregory's *Chronicle* [4]

London.   *c.* 1451–2.

1423. . . . Also thys tyme alle tho that benne in the
same strenghthe or brygge [5] of Mylanke, that have or
holdyn, or that othyr holdyn in hyr behalfe, any towne,
place, or strengythe, dysobeysauns to oure lorde the Kyng [6]
and my sayde lorde the Regaunt,[7] delyvyr and yelde hem
up unto my sayde lorde or to hys deputys. And with that

---

[1] Devotional exercises; discussions on a text from the Scriptures,
etc.   [2] Covered.   [3] Collects.

[4] Part of the terms of the treaty of surrender after the siege of
Pont Melaun, between the town and the English.

[5] Bridge fortress.   [6] Henry VI.   [7] Duke of Bedford.

they shalle doo alle hyr myght and trewe devyr an gayne hyr parentes and frendys,[1] yf any there bene, that holde any suche strengythe or towne dysobeysauns, that they shulle yeldyin hem up to my sayde lorde, etc. . . . the whiche thyng above sayde and done and fullefylle[d] dewly, he shall ressayve hem as hyt ys above sayde.

Also yf any be in the same sayde brygge or strengythe of Melancke, havyn and holdyn,[2] in what [place] that they bene, any presoners, be they Fraynysche, Englysche, Burgonys [3] or othyr, of the oboysauns or servyse of owre lorde the Kyng, and of my lorde the Regaunt, they shalle yoldyn [4] hem and delyvery hem frely and quytly, with owte takyng of the sayde personys or of hyr pleggys any fynaunce [5] or ramsomys. . . .

And in the monythe of Apprylle was made the allyaunce by twyne the Regaunt of Fraunce, the Duke of Bedforde, the Duke of Burgayne,[6] and the Duke of Bretayne. . . .

From William Gregory's *Chronicle*

London.   *c.* 1451–2.

1360. . . . The same yere Kyng Edwarde saylyd into Fraunce, by cause that Charlys Regaynt of Fraunce hadde movyd and steryd warre a gayne the Kynge of Inglonde. And the same yere of oure Lorde M[l]cccx ande the xiiij day of Aprylle, the morne aftyr Estyr daye that yere, the kynge with hys hoste lay aboute Parys. And that day was a foule derke day of myste, rayne, and hayle, and soo bytter colde that men dyde [7] for cold, where fore yet in to thys day hyt ys i-callyd Blacke Monday next aftyr Estyr day.

---

[1] Relations.   [2] Having and holding.   [3] Burgundians (Bourgognes).
[4] Yield, hand over.   [5] Fine.   [6] Burgundy (Bourgogne).   [7] Died.

1361. Ande that yere were rovers apon the see undyr the governayle of the Erle of Syn Poule.[1] And the fyrste day of Marche they dystryde [2] the Rye and Hastynge [3] ande many moo townys by the see syde, and slowe many menne. And that yere the pesse was made by twyne Kynge Edwarde and Kyng John of Fraunce, the x day of May. The Kyng of Inglond sende hys bassetours [4] to take the othe of the Regayunt of Fraunce, Charlys, the whiche othe was doo undyr this forme: Charlys dyd do syng a masse solempny [5]; and whenne that Agnus Dei was thryesse i-sayde layde his ryght honde uppon the patent,[6] were uppo lay Goddys owne precyus body, and his lyfte honde on the Masse Boke, sayng on thys wyse, 'We sweryng uppon this holy precyus Goddys body, and uppon the Ewangelys [7] fermly and trewly to holdyn and mentayne pesse and concorde by twyne us two kynges, and in no maner for to do the contrarye in no maner wyse.' And that same yere men, bestys, treys, and howsys were smyght fervently with lytthenyge, and sodenly i-peryschyde. And they fonde [8] in mannys lyckenys splatt[9] men goyng in the waye.

From William Gregory's *Chronicle*

London.   *c.* 1451–2.

1333. And that same yere the kyng of Schotlonde [10] came to the Newe Castelle uppon Tynde. And at the feste of Syn John the Baptyste he did omage unto oure Kyng of

---

[1] St. Pol.   [2] Destroyed.   [3] Two of the Cinque ports.
[4] Ambassadors.
[5] Caused or commanded a solemn mass to be sung.
[6] Paten.   [7] Gospels.   [8] The fiend.
[9] Cut open, butchered (ME. *splatten*).
[10] Edward Balliol.

Inglonde.[1] And the same yere the Duke of Bretayne [2] dyde omage to the kynge for the Counte of Regemounde,[3] the yere of our Lorde M[l]cccxxxiij.

1334. And that yere was grete dethe of men and morayne of bestys and grete rayne. And that yere a quarter of whete was worth xj schelyngys. . . .

1336. And that same yere, in the mounthis of Junij and Julij, in dyvers partys of hevyn apperyde the starre comate, *id est* a blasyng sterre. And that yere was grete plenty of vytayle, and a quarter whete was at ij s. at London, and a fat oxe for vj s. viij d., and vj pejonys [4] for a peny; nevyrtheles ther was grete scharsyte of mony that tyme. Al so that yere deyde Syr John of Eltham. Alle so the kyng grauntyd that yere that the sargentys of the mayre and sherevys schulde bere by fore them macys of sylver and ovyr gylte with the kyngys armys in that one ende and the armys of London in that othyr ende.

From AGNES PASTON,
                To her son, JOHN PASTON

Norfolk.   *c.* 1451.

I grete yow wele, and lete yow wete that on the Sonday befor Sent Edmond,[5] after evyn songe, Augnes Ball com to me to my closett [6] and bad me good evyn, and Clement Spycer with hyr. And I acsyd hym what he wold? And he askyd me why I had stoppyd in [7] the Kyngs wey? And I seyd to hym I stoppyd no wey butt myn owyn, and askyd hym why he had sold my lond to John Ball? And he sor [8] he was nevyr a cordyd with your fadyr; and I told hym if

---

[1] Edward III.   [2] Duke of Brittany.   [3] Richmond.
[4] Pigeons.   [5] St. Edmund's day was 16th November.   [6] Pew.
[7] Built (a wall) over.   [8] Swore.

hys fadyr had do as he dede, he wold be a chamyd to a seyd
as he seyd.   And all that tyme Waryn Herman lenyd ovyr
the parklos [1] and lystynd what we seyd, and seyd that the
chaunge was a rewly chaunge, for the towne was un do
therby, and is the werse by an c li.   And I told hym it
was no curtese to medyll hym in a mater butt if he wer
callyd to councell; and prowdly goyn [2] forthe with me in
the cherche, he seyd the stoppyng of the wey xuld coste me
xx nobylls, and ʒet it shuld downe ageyn.   And I lete
hym wete he that putte it downe chull pay therfor.   Also
he seyd it was well don that I sett men to werke to owle [3]
meney whyll I was her, butt in the ende I chale lese my
coste. . . .

Wretyn at Paston, on the day after Sent Edmond.

Be yowyr modyr,

AUGNES PASTON.

The Paston Letters.

From MARGARET PASTON,

To her husband, JOHN PASTON

Norfolk.   *25th Nov.* 1455.

Right wurshipfull husbonde, I recomaunde me unto you.
Plesith you to witte that myn aunt Mondeforthe [4] hath
desiryd me to write to you, besechyng you that ye wol
wochsafe [5] to chevesshe [6] for her at London xx[tl] marke
for to be payed to Mastre Ponyngs, outher on Saterday or
Sonday, weche schalbe Seint Andrwes Daye, in discharchyng of them that be bounden to Mastre Ponyngs of the

---

[1] i.e. the half-door of the pew.   [2] Going.

[3] ? To oil (the palms).

[4] Wife of Osbert Moundford of Hockwold, and daughter of
John Berney.

[5] Vouchsafe.   [6] Purchase, exchange.

s[ei]de xx^{ti} marke for the wardeship of her doughter, the weche xx^{ti} marke she hath delyvered to me in golde for you to have at your comyng home, for she dare not aventure her money to be brought up to London for feere of robbyng; for it is seide heere that there goothe many thefys be twyx this and London, weche causeth her to beseche you to content [1] the seide money in dischargyng of the matre, and of them that be bounden, for she wolde for no goude that the day were broken.   And she thankyth you hertely for the greet labour and besynesse that ye have had in that matre, and in all others touchyng her and hers, wherfore she seithe she is ever bounden to be your bedwoman [2] and ever wolle be whyle she levethe.

My cosyn, her sone, and hese wife recomaundethe them unto you, besechyng you that ye woll weche safe to be her goode mastre, as ye have ben a fore tyme; for they be enformed that Danyell is comen to Rysyng Castell, and hes men make her [3] bost that her mastre shal be a yene at Brayston withinne shorte tyme. . . .

Wreten at Norweche, on Seint Kateryn Day.

Be your,

MARGARET PASTON.

The Paston Letters.

From THOMAS BOURCHIER, Archbishop of Canterbury,
    To SIR JOHN FASTOLF

London.   26th *March* 1456.

Right worshipful, and my right entierly welbeloved, I grete you right hertely wele, thanking you specialy, and in full herty wise for the verray geantle goodnesse that ye have shewid unto me at all tymes, praying you of good contynuance.

[1] Pay in full.   [2] Well-wisher, true friend.   [3] Their.

And as touching suche matiers as ye sente unto me fore, I truste to God verraly, insomuche as the rule is amendid heer, and the wedder waxeth seesonable and pleasante, to see you in thise parties within short tyme, at whiche tyme I shal commune and demeene unto you in suche wise,[1] that ye shal be right wele pleasid.

And as for the matier concernyng my Lord of Bedford, thinketh nat contrarye, but that ye shal finde me hertly welwillid to doo that I can or may for thaccomplesshment of youre desire, as wel in that matier as in other, like as your servaunte John Bokking, berer hereof, can clierlier reporte unto you on my behalve; to whom like hit you to yeve feith and credence in this partie.   And the blissid Trinitee have you everlastingly in His keping.

Written in my Manoir of Lamehith,[2] the xxvj daie of March.

Your feithfull and trew,

Th. Cant.

The Paston Letters.

From Margaret Paston,

To her husband, John Paston

Norfolk.   *29th April* 1459.

Rythe worchepfwl hosbond, I recommawnd me onto yow.   Plesyth you to wete that on Thorisday last was ther wer browt unto this towne many Prevy Selis,[3] and on of hem was indosyd to yow, and to Hastynggs, and to fyve or sexe odyr gentylmen; and anodyr was sent onto yowr sone, and indosyd to hym selfe alone, and asynyd wythinne wyth

---

[1] Discuss with you, and so conduct myself and the matter . . .
[2] Lambeth.   [3] i.e. here a royal summons to military service.

the Kynggys howyn hand, and so wer bwt fewe that wer sent, as it was told me; and also ther wer mor specyal teryms in hys then wern in oderys.   I sey [1] a copy of thoo that wer sent onto odyr gentylmen.   The intent of the wrytyng was, that they sshuwlde be wyth the Kyngg at Leycester the x day of May, wyth as many personys defensebylly arayid as they myte acordyng to her degre, and that they schwld bryng wyth hem for her expensys for ij monythis. . . .

I prey yow that ye vowchesaf to send word in hast how ye wyl that yor sone be demenyd herin.   Men thynk her, that ben yowr wel wyllerys, that ye may no lesse do than to send hym forthe. . . .[2]

As for alle odyr tynggys [3] at hom, I hope that I and odyr schal do howr part ther inne, as well as we may, bwt as for mony, it comyth bwt slowly.   And God have yow in hys kepyng, and sen yow good sped in alle yowr matteris.

Wretyn in hast at Norwece, on the Sonday next before the Assencyon Day.

Ser, I wold be ryte glad to he [4] swmme gode tydynggys fro yow.

Be yorys,

M. P.

The Paston Letters.

From a PETITION OF THE PARISHIONERS OF DIDCOT, TO THOMAS STONOR

Didcot (Oxon).   *c.* 1465.

Besechethe lowly and mekely unto youre gracious

[1] Saw.

[2] At the time, Edward Paston, John's son, had displeased his father, and was in disgrace.   [3] Things.   [4] Hear.

Maistership youre pore bedemen and tenauntes off youre lordeship off Dudcote, wich beth gretly wronged and ungodely entreted by the parson off Dudcote foresaid: wich parson desired off the Township foresaid . . . to go to scole to Oxonford, and the said parson to fynde his depute and his attorney for alle sacramentes and necessaries in his absence there treuly to be observed and kept. Herapon this was graunted to the said parson, and then the parson yeed [1] to Oxford, and the dyvyne service and other sacramentes wer not kept as thei aght [2] to be, to gret unese [3] to the parish. Ferthermore the chirchemen of Dudcote wer in bargenyng of a ryke off weete [4] for the welfare and help off the chirch: the seid parson undirstode this, and unkyndly labored to Doctor Bulkley, that was awner off the reke, and prively bargened with [him] and put the chirchemen aparte. And when the parson com home he declared in the polepitt openly, that it was the Doctor wille the parissh shuld by [5] the straw off the reke, because thei had but litell stuff among hem this yere: God knoweth full evell penyworthes thei had and sharp. . . . Also, the said parson yeed to Oxonford, and graunted to Williham Harries a dayes thress [6] off straw off the same for ix d. And he remembred him, and wold not let him have it after under xvj d. a daies thress, and ever sold so and derrer.[7] . . . Item, Robert Dobson, the parsons man, repreved and ungodely in the moost unhonest wise called diverse men knaves, and harlettes and charles,[8] . . . and the said parson mayntened him therein. Thei wer so bold that tweyne off the parsons men lay

---

[1] Yede [OE. *eode*], went. [2] Ought.
[3] Distress, inconvenience.
[4] Rick of wheat. [5] Buy.
[6] Day's thresh.
[7] Dearer. [8] Churls.

awayte apon John Pepwite in Bagley, and ther thei bete him and except pepull of Abendon,[1] likly to have kylled [him].

The Stonor Letters and Papers.

From various accounts in the STONOR PAPERS

Stonor (Oxon).   *c.* 1466–71.

c. 1466.

In primis,   spende at Illysley when ye rode yn to Deveneshyre. ij d.

Item,   at Ermyngton for wosshyng of yowyr shertys and M. Wyllyams, iij d.

Item,   when y rode to seke M. Sakvyle, spende at Abyndon, iij d.

Item,   for ij chekons both [2] at Wodestok for yowre hawkys, ij d.

Item,   yn yowre drynkyng when ye wente a hawkyng at Wodestoke ij d.

Item,   for a payre hosyn for M. Mary ij d.

Item,   a cappe for M. Isabell ij d. ob.

October 1468—July 1469.

for   the showyng of xij oxyne. v s.

for   a servys of Trenchers. iiij d.

for   ij pygkys, viij d.
a shert for Richard, viij d.

for   half a foote a cloutyng ledyr, iiij d.
saltefyhs and saltesamon, vij d.

to   Raulyn Clerke for the eryng [3] of xij akyrs londe in lityll Derrabut fyld, xij s. iiij d.

---

[1] Had it not been for the people of Abingdon.
[2] Bought.   [3] Ploughing.

1469–71.

Item,   paid to a thetcher, thetchyng on the berne be
xiij dayes, takyng a day iij d., iij s. iij d.

Item,   a peyre of shoyn [1] for Maister Edmund, vj d.

Item,   payed when my seyde master and mastresse
went to Cawyrsame for drynkyng at watter
syde, iij d.

From MARGARET PASTON,

To her son, SIR JOHN PASTON

Norfolk.   29*th Oct.* 1466.

I grytte you well, and send you God ys blessyng, and
myn, desyryng you to send me werd how that ye spede in
youre maters, for I thynk ryght leng tyll I here tydyngys
from you; and in alwyse I avyse you for to be ware that ye
kepe wysly your wrytyngys that ben of charge,[2] that it
com not in her [3] handys that may hurt you herafter.
Your fader, wham God assole,[4] in hys trobyll seson set more
by hys wrytyngs and evydens than he dede by any of hys
moveabell godys. . . .

Item, I wold ye shold take hyde that yf any processe com
owte a yenst me, or a yenst any of tho that wer endyted a
fore the coroner, that I myght have knowlych therof, and
to purvey a remedy therfor. . . .

And at the reverens of God, spede your maters so thys
terme, that we may be in rest herafter, and lette [5] not for
no labour for the season, and remember the grete cost and
charge that we have had hedyr toward,[6] and thynk verely
it may not lenge endur.   Ye know what ye left when ye

---

[1] Shoon, shoes.   [2] That are important.   [3] Their.
[4] Assoil.   [5] Delay.   [6] Hitherto

E

wer last at hom, and wyte it verely there ys no more in thys countray to bere owte no charge with. I awyse you enquer wysely yf ye canne gyte any more ther as[1] ye be, for els by my feth I feer els it will not be well with ous; and send me word in hast hough ye doo. . . .

Wryten at Caster,[2] the moreu next after Symon and Jude, wher as I wold not be at thys tyme but for your sake, so mot I ches.[3]

By your Moder.

The Paston Letters.

From JOHN YEME,

To THOMAS STONOR

Stonor (and London).   11*th June, c.* 1466.

Rygth Reverent Mayster, y recomand me unto yowe, desyryng to here of yower wellefare, and prosperyte of body and sawle, beseking Almyȝthy Jhesu preservy hit unto his plesure and to yower worly[4] worschyppe and herte ys desyre. . . .

Fudermore, Walter Frende recomandes hym to yower good maisterchyppe, and he wolle pray yowe to sende hym worde wher[5] to Mylle of Ermyngton schall be y-koweryn[6] with stone or strawe, and wher he schall ordeyne[7] any haye ayenst yower coming. Y wold have come home to your maisterchyppe, but y have y-taryd vij dayys yn London apon you: for the osteler tellyd me that ye wolde have y-be ther atte the begynnyng of the terme. All so y have y-bofte[8] me a hors atte London, for y loste my hors

---

[1] Where.   [2] Caister.
[3] If I had my choice (lit. 'so might I choose').
[4] Worldly.   [5] Whether.   [6] Covered, roofed.
[7] Provide.   [8] Bought.

ful falsly and untreuly apon the waye, as I tryste to Godde to enforme yower maysterchyppe. . . .

All so Ric. Fortescu ffaryth ffowle with Walter Frende and me, and layyth his men yn awayte to murder me . . . and all ys for by cawse y wolde notte suffry hym to have his yntente at Plympton Corte; . . . And as for the Corte of Tremeton,[1] y have mycche laburr ther; but yette y have notte geffe [2] no ple [3] ther, for he ys asoynyd [4] ij tymys a rewe [5] yn his oune pleynte.   And that sawe y never yn no place but ther. . . . No more to yowe atte thys tyme. And Jhesu preservy yow yn his blessyd kepyng.   Amen.

Y-wrytyn atte London on Seynte Barnabe y Evyn [6] yn all haste.

By yower pore servant,

JOHN YEME.

The Stonor Letters and Papers.

From THOMAS ROKES,

To his brother-in-law, THOMAS STONOR

Stonor (and Ascot).   1st Oct. 1467.

Rygth worshypfull Syr, and my rygth Good Brodyr, aftyr all dew recommendasyon had, I recomawnd me unto yow, to my Mastres, my dowter, and to all my young Cosyngs,[7] the weche I pray God to preserve and kepe for his mersy; and I ame sory that my horse servyd yow no better: and yf he mowghth [8] have plesyd yow for a yoman to have redyn on, I wold have holdyn me rygth well content and ye had kepyd hyme styll: but I trust in God I schall purvey yow of a lytyll hors soche as ye schall com

---

[1] Trematon.   [2] Given.   [3] Plea.   [4]Assigned.
[5] Twice in succession.   [6] Even.   [7] Cousins.   [8] Might.

and thanke for.   And I send yow yowr hors by the brynger of thys letter, yowr servant: he wyll not be in pleyte [1] as I wold have hyme, but he ys both herty and hoole: God save hyme.   And hyt lyke yow, ye send me word how my Nawnte [2] is disposyd, now the dettes be payd, to performe my Nonkilles [3] wyll, hoys [4] sowle God pardon.   I beseche you as for my Nowntes [2] surte [5] and myn that ye wyll comyn [6] hyt with sum leryd [7] body for the surte of us both acordyng to his wyll.   And I schall old [8] me rygth well content. . . . I have a lytyll besynes yet in my hervyst: as sone as I cane ryd [9] that, I schall se both yow and my Nawnt with Godes Grase, whome evyr preserve yow and yowrs for his mersy.   Wretyn at Ascot on Satyrday next after Mykaellmes day.

By yowr Brodyr,
Thomas Rokes.

The Stonor Letters and Papers.

From Jane Stonor,

To her husband, Thomas Stonor

Stonor (Oxon).   c. 1470.

Syr, I recommande me unto yow as lowly as I cane: pleseyt yow to wyte I have ressevyde a byle [10] frome yow wherby I undyrstonde My lorde Morlay [11] dissyres to sugiorne [12] with yow: what answere þat ye have ȝevyn hym I cannot undyrstond be your bylle: I soposse your mynid was apon sum odyr materys when þat ye wrotyt,[13] bot and

---

[1] Plight, condition.   [2] Aunt, < min aunte.
[3] Uncle, < min unkel.   [4] Whose.   [5] Surety.
[6] Discuss.   [7] Learned.   [8] Hold.   [9] Rid.
[10] Bill, letter.   [11] Morley.   [12] Sojourn, stay.   [13] Wrote it.

ye have not granttyde, I beseke yow to aschusyt,[1] and to
contend your litylle abyddynge at home, and allso þe
joberde [2] of yowr chelder [3] and of all your howys [4] at your
hasty goyng in to Devenscheyr: for and your abyddyng at
home be no nodyrwyse þan yt ys, þat wolle be [non]e
profete unto yow, and hertes ese unto me: raythere breke
up housallde [5] þan take sugiornantes, for servantes be not
so delygent as þei were wonto bee.   Now, farewelle, good
syr, and Gode ȝeve yow goode nyghte and brynge yow
welle home in schorte tyme.   Wrytyn at Stonor apon
Sante Symon and Judes daye at eve.

Be your awne

JAYN STONOR.

The Stonor Letters and Papers.

From SIR JOHN PASTON,

      To his brother, JOHN PASTON

Norfolk.   *March* 1470.

I comande me to yow, etc. . . .

    Item, as for Mestresse Kateryn Dudle,[6] I have many
tymes recomandyd yow to hyr, and she is noo thynge
displeasyd with itt.   She rekkythe not howe many gentylmen love hyr; she is full of love.   I have betyn the mater
for yow, your onknowleche,[7] as I told hyr.   She answerythe
me, that sche woll noon thys ij yer, and I beleve hyr; for I
thynke sche hathe the lyffe that sche can holde hyr content
with; I trowe she woll be a sore laboryng woman this ij
yer for mede of hyr sowle. . . . Item, ther is comen a newe
litell Torke, whyche is a wele vysagyd felawe, off the age

---

[1] Excuse it, decline it   [2] Jeopardy.   [3] Children.   [4] House.
[5] Household.   [6] Dudley.   [7] Without your knowledge.

off xl yere; and he is lower than Manuell by a hanffull, and lower then my lytell Tom by the schorderys, and mor lytell above hys pappe; and he hathe, as he seyde to the Kynge [1] hymselffe iii or iiij sonys, chyldre, iche one off hem as hyghe and asse lykly as the Kynge hymselffe; and he is leggyd right i-now, and it is reportyd that hys pyntell is as long as hys legge.

Item, I praye yow schewe, or rede to my moodre such thynges as ye thynke is for her to know, afftre yowr dyscression. . . .

J. P., K.

The Paston Letters.

From   Warkworth's [2] *Chronicle*

Oct. 1470.

Here is to knowe that in the begynnynge of the moneth of Octobre, the yere of oure Lorde, a M.CCCC.LXX, the Bisshoppe of Wynchestere be the assent of the Duke of Clarence and the Erle of Warwyke went to the toure of Londone where Kynge Herry was in presone by Kynge Edwardes commawndement, and there toke hyme from his kepers, whiche [3] was noȝt worschipfully arayed as a prince, and noȝt so clenly kept as schuld seme [4] suche a Prynce; thei hade hym oute and newe arayed hym, and dyde to hyme grete reverens, and brought hyme to the palys of Westmynster, and so he was restorede to the crowne ageyne . . . whereof alle his goode lovers [5] were fulle gladde, and the more parte of peple.   Nevere the lattere before that at he was putt oute of his reame by Kynge Edwarde, alle Eng-

---

[1] Edward IV.

[2] John Warkworth, Master of St. Peter's College, Cambridge.

[3] Who.   [4] Become.   [5] Friends, supporters.

londe for the more party hated hym, and were fulle gladde
to have a chounge [1]; and the cause was the good Duke of
Glouceter was put to deth and Jhon Holande, Duke of
Excetre poysond, and that the Duke of Suffolke, the Lord
Say, Danyelle Trevyliane and other myscheves people that
were aboute the Kynge were so covetouse toward them selff
and dyd no force of the Kynges honour, ne of his wele, ne
of the comone wele of the londe where Kynge Herry trusted
to them that thei schuld do. . . .

From *The Historie of the Arrival of King Edward IV*

c. 1471.

And, for it was right derke, and he [2] myght not well se
where his enemyes were enbatayled afore him, he lodged
hym and all his hoste [3] afore them moche nere then he had
supposed, but he toke nat his ground so even in the front
afore them as he wold have don yf he might bettar have
sene them, butt somewhate a-syden-hande, where he disposed all his people in good arraye all that nyght; and so
they kept them still, withowt any mannar langwage or
noyse but as lytle as they well myght. Bothe parties had
goons and ordinaunce, but thErle of Warwike had many
moo then the Kynge, and therefore, on the nyght, weninge
gretly to have anoyed the Kinge, and his hooste with shot
of gonnes, thErls fielde shotte gunes almoste all the nyght.
But thanked be God it so fortuned that they alway ovar-
shote the Kyngs hoste and hurtyd them nothinge and the
cawse was the Kyngs hoste lay muche nerrar them than
they demyd. And with that also the Kyng and his hoste
kept passinge great silence alnyght and made as who saythe
no noyse, whereby they might nat know the very place

---

[1] Change.   [2] Edward IV.   [3] i.e. on the field of Barnet.

where they lay. And for that they shulde not know it; the Kynge suffred no gonns to be shote on his syd all that nyght, or els right fewe whiche was to hym great advauntage, for therby they myght have estemed the ground that he lay in and have leveled theire gunns nere.

From EDMUND STONOR,

To his brother, WILLIAM STONOR

Stonor (Oxon).   *c.* 1475.

My rygth wurschypfull Brothyr, I recommaund me unto yow, desyryng to her[1] off your wellfare, the qwyhych[2] almyghty [Jhesu] contynw: doyng yow to wytt that John Blakall browtt to Stonor a dyker[3] for to make yowr dykes in [So and So] feld, betwen the hy way[4] and the ew[5] tre: and John Mathew and I wolde a mad a bargeyn with hym, but we [cowd] nott styll[6] there on, nedyr we wyst nott how ye wold have hytt; whedyr ye wold have hytt sengyll dydge[7] or [dobyll] dydge, and therffor we mad no bargeyn with hym; but I askyd hym how he wold do a perdge[8] of sempyll[9] dydge, and for [so many] d. he wold a don hytt a dobyll, sett hym[10] with whit thorn, and a mad the dydge a yerd deppe: and yff hytt wold plesse yow to [send] word to John or to me whedyr ye wold have hytt dobyll dydge or senkyll, and what ye wull geve for a perdge, we [wull] send for hym. . . . And also, brothyr, wher ye speke to B . . ., carpenter, so to make yowr myll hows, he sayeth he can nott make hytt, but he mak hytt new; but Wyllyam Ale . . . wyk [sayeth] that [he] with thyn lytyll space

[1] Hear.   [2] Which.   [3] Dyker, one who made ditches.
[4] Highway.   [5] Yew.   [6] Decide.   [7] Ditch.
[8] Perch.   [9] Simple, i.e. single.   [10] i.e. it.

wyll mak ye þat hows to stand ther xx yere, and okapy [1]
but lytyll new tymbyre: and we thy[nk] hyt wer þe lestt
schardge [2] to yow so, thane to mak a new hows.   But I
beseche yow, brothyr, latt not yowr carpenter know þat
I send yow thys now.   No more to yow brothyr, at thys
tyme. . . .

Your brothyr,

S

EDMUND ROT

N

The Stonor Letters and Papers.

From THOMAS BETSON,

> To KATHERINE RYCHE

Stonor (Oxon).   *1st June* 1476.

My nowne hartely belovid Cossen Kateryn,[3] I recomande
me unto yow withe all the inwardnesse of myn hart.   And
now lately ye shall understond þat I resseyvid a token ffrom
yow, the which was and is to me right hartely welcom . . .
and over that I had a letter ffrom Holake, youre gentyll
Sqwyer, by the which I understond right well þat ye be in
good helth off body, and mery at hart.   And I pray God
hartely to his plesour to contenew the same: ffor it is to me
veray grete comfforth þat ye so be, so helpe me Jhesu.
And yff ye wold be a good etter [4] off your mete allwaye,
that ye myght waxe and grow ffast to be a woman, ye
shuld make me the gladdest man off the world, be my
trouth: [5] ffor whanne I remembre your ffavour and your

---

[1] 'Occupy,' use.   [2] The least charge, expense.
[3] A little girl of about twelve, great-granddaughter of Wm.
Gregory (see p. 39f).   Betson married her in 1478.
[4] Eater.   [5] Troth.

sadde loffynge delynge to me wardes, ffor south ye make me evene veray glade and joyus in my hart; and on the toþer-syde agayn, whanne I remembre your yonge youthe, and seeth [1] well that ye be none eteter off youre mete, the which shuld helpe you greately in waxynge, ffor south þan ye make me veray hevy agayn. And therffore I praye you, myn nown swete Cossen, evene as you loffe me, to be mery and to eate your mete lyke a woman. And yff ye so will do ffor my loveff,[2] looke what ye will desyre off me, what-somever it be, . . . I promesse you by the helpe of our Lord to perfforme it to my power . . . and over that I send you the blissynge þat our Lady gaveffe [3] hir dere sonne, and ever well to ffare. I pray you grete well my horsse, and praye him to gyffe yow iiij off his yeres [4] to helpe you with all: and I will at my comynge home gyff hym iiij off my yeres and iiij horsse lofes till amendes.[5] . . .

And Almyghty Jhesu make you a good woman and send you many good yeres and longe to lyveffe. . . .

At greate Cales on this syde on the see, the ffyrst day off June, whanne every man was gone to his Dener, and the Cloke smote noynne,[6] and all oure howsold cryed after me and badde me come down, 'Come down to dener at ones!' and what answer I gaveffe hem ye know it off old.

Be your ffeiȝthefull Cossen and loffer,

THOMAS BETSON.

I sent [7] you this rynge ffor a token.

The Stonor Letters and Papers.

---

[1] See.   [2] Love (sb.).   [3] Gave (gaveth).   [4] Years.
     [5] Loaves, as a reward.   [6] Noon.   [7] Send.

From Caxton's *History of the Life of Jason*

London. *c.* 1477.

And howe be it that myn auctor [1] writeth that he hath
founde nomore of thistorie [2] of Iason, yet haue I founden
and red in the boke that Bochace [3] made . . . that whan
so was that Iason and Medea were reconciled agayn to
geder, after that shee fled from Egeon, that he went with
her into Colchos again, and whan he was comen theder, he
founde the olde king Oetes, fader vnto Medea, banissed
and exiled out of his royame, whom he restored . . . and
also he [3] saith that Thoant and Euneus where [4] his sones
whom he begate on Ysiphile, as he went to Colchos where
as Stacius saith, Whiche were born at ones. And for
asmoch as it was not the custome in Lenos to fede and
norisshe the men children, they were sent into an other
countrey for to be nourysshed, wherfore the moder was put
out of her Royaume and taken with pirates and theues,
and after sold vnto Lygurgis, king of Nemee; and after
whan the sayde sones waxe [5] men, they went with king
Adrastus vnto the bataile of Thebes, and as they went in
the wode of Nemee they herde of the sayd king Adrastus
reherse her burth [6] and the caas [7] of her moder, by which
rehersayll they knew that she was their moder.

From Caxton's *History of the Life of Jason*

London. *c.* 1477.

Than that [8] Corfus the right Cruell geant had vnderstand [9] the wordes of Iason, he lefte [10] vp his heed and chyn,

[1] i.e. Raoul Le Fevre. [2] The historie, i.e. the tale, or story.
[3] Boccaccio. [4] Were. [5] Grew (to be). [6] Their birth.
[7] Story. [8] When. [9] Understood. [10] Lifted.

alle chargid with heer like a Beer [1]; and after enhaunced [2] his trenchaunt swerd with a grete Corage [3] right angry, and smote Iason and gaf hym so terryble and poyssaunt [4] stroke, that he bare a way more than a grete quarter of his shelde.   And when Iason felte him so smeton [5] of the Geant, he lefte vp his swerd a heyght [6] wher with he araught [7] his mortel ennemy vpon the coppe [8] of his helme, in employeng [9] alle his might, that the Geant was constrayned to enclyne his heed alle lowe.   Wherof many had grete meruayle.

As ye may Vnderstonde, the two Champyons began to entretaste [10] eche other with their trenchaunt swerdes. Alle way the geant, after that he had receyuid this peysaunt [11] strook, he haunced [12] his hand with his swerd agayn and supposed [13] to haue smeton Iason. . . . But Iason sette litil therby, Sauyng he began a lytil to smyle and lawhe [14]; And if he was glad, so were they of Olyferne, that beheld the bataylle of the two champyons.   But hit was not long after but their lawhynges changed into wepynges. For the geant, as all despayred, Ran vpon Iason so eygrely [15] that he wist not how to saue him, on that other syde he sawe hys shelde all in pieces.   And with that he gaf him a wounde vpon the lyfte [16] syde, that the blood ran doun fro the wounde largely.

[1] Bear (sb.).   [2] Lifted up.   [3] Spirit.
[4] Powerful.   [5] Smitten.   [6] On high.
[7] Smote.   [8] Top.   [9] Employing.
[10] Deal each other blows.   [11] Powerful, cf. poyssaunt.
[12] Cf. enhanced.   [13] Thought.   [14] Laugh.
[15] Angrily.   [16] Left.

From THOMAS HENHAM,
    To SIR WILLIAM STONOR

Stonor (Oxon).   *16th July* 1478.

Ryght Reverent and worshypffull mayster, I recommaunde me unto your goode maystershype, ever more desyryng to here off your goode wellfare, . . . Forder more your mayster [1] schalle understonde that I sende dow[n]e by John Talbose, your sarvaynte: Itm. your demy gowne of chamelet [2]; Itm. your demy gowne off blake pewke [3] lynde with grene wellffete,[4] truste [5] in a shete. Forder more, Syr, ye shall understonde that masterys Hane [6] hys [7] well amendyde, blesyde by Jhesu, and hys in goode hallthe.[8] Forder more, Syr, your maystershype shall understonde that the hale [9] brewer callys apone me dayly sore ffore monay, the wyche I have wretyn unto your maysterschype affor tyme, the Somma [10] ys v li . . . the whyche he besekys your maysterschype that he mythe have some monay in hande unto the tyme that your maysterschype come unto London. All so, Syr, I beseke your maysterschype þat ye wylle remember your brede [11] baker at London, ffor he callys apone me daylle [12] ffor monay, the wyche some hys xxxv s. and iiij d. No more unto your maysterschype at thys tyme, butt all mythy Jhesu have you in hys kepyng. Wretyn at London the xvj day off Jullii.

         By your prentes,[13]

               THOMAS HENHAM.
            The Stonor Letters and Papers.

[1] i.e. your maysterschype.
[2] At that time=hair-cloth made from Angora goat.
[3] Superior woollen cloth.   [4] Velvet.   [5] 'Trussed,' packed.
[6] Mistress Anne Ryche, Katherine's sister, see p. 53.
[7] Is.   [8] Health.   [9] Ale.   [10] i.e. summa.   [11] Bread.
[12] Daily.   [13] Apprentice,

From RICHARD CELY, the Elder,[1]

To his son, GEORGE CELY.

Essex and London.   25*th* Aug. 1478.

I grete the [2] wyll, and I have resayvyd from the a lecter [3] wryte at Caleys, the xiij day of Auguste, the weche lecter I have wyll understande, and ye have solde vj sarplerys [4] of my good cottyswolde woll, pryse the sacke xix marke to Peter van de Rade, and Danyell van de Rade, marchantys of Bregys.[5] . . . I understand ye have resayvyd my woll late schepyt,[6] xlvij sarplerys and a poke,[7] all Cottyswolde, and my fell [8] in savete, I thanke God, and the frayght [9] payd, for the weche I pray yow send me a cope of the payyng of the frayfte,[9] that I may wryt in my bogke the passelys; [10] and for the costom and subsete,[11] pay hyt as hoder [12] men doe. . . .

I pray the make salle to sure men [13] and ye can, for the warled ys not good; were for, it ys as good for to lese [14] in the bege[n]yng as in the ende.   Save as meche as ye may for the exschange, be [l]yche [15] it wyll be hevy to bare, the weche I pray God ament hyt. . . .

per RYCHARD CELY.

The Cely Papers.

---

[1] The Celys were merchants of the wool staple at Calais and London.   Perhaps of Cornish origin, but owned land in and lived in Aveley in Essex.   Well-to-do and mercenary.   Richard the elder was head of the family.

[2] Thee.   [3] Letter.   [4] Sacks (measure).
[5] Bruges.   [6] Lately shipped.   [7] Bag (measure).
[8] Whole skins with wool left on.
[9] freight.   [10] Details, items, particulars.
[11] Subsidy.   [13] Other.
[13] Sell to trustworthy men.   [14] Lose.   [15] 'Belike,' probably.

From DAME ELIZABETH STONOR,

    To her husband, SIR WILLIAM STONOR

Stonor (Oxon).   *Oct. 5th* 1478.

Right best and hartely well belovid husbond, I recommaund me unto you with all myn hart, lettynge you wete
that I am right well amendid, I thannke god þeroff; and
on Sonday last past I was at the chirche at my ffadyrs
deryge,[1] and soppid with my modyr the same nyght.   And
Syr, yeff I had ones done my pilgramages [2] I reke nat how
sone I were with you at Stonor: and þerffore, gentyll Syr,
I praye you þat ye ffayll nat to send me myn horsse on
Settyrday next. . . . And also I praye you to remembre
my sonne Betson; ffor he hath mych adoo with money now,
and he trustith veraly to your promesse. . . .

My modyr and my broodyr Stooker recomaunde hem
both right hartely unto you . . . truly I am veray wery
off London, ffor my son Betson intendes to ryde in to the
countre, now whenne I come home; and he is fast ryggynge
hym [3] þer ffore, so that at many tymes I am post a loyne,[4]
and that causeth me to thynnke the more ellynger [5]: and
þerffore, good Syr, remembre myn horsse on Setterday with
owte ffawte. . . .

God lenne [6] grace, who preserve you ever in vertu
and longe helth to Godes plesour.   The v day off
Octobre.

            By your ovne wyff,

                D. ELYSABETH STONORE.

               The Stonor Letters and Papers.

---

[1] My father's dirige, i.e. the mass in anniversary of his death.

[2] She had probably vowed to go on pilgrimage to certain shrines
when she was ill.

[3] Preparing himself.   [4] 'Post alone,' utterly alone.

[5] Comp. of ellynge, elenge=sorrowfully.   [6] Give.

From GEORGE CELY,

To his father, RICHARD CELY, the Elder

Essex and London. 16th Nov. 1480.

Ryght rewerent and worshypffull Fadyr, affter all dewe
recomendacyon pretendyng, I recomeawnd me unto yow
in the moste lowlyest whisse that I con or may . . .

Ther ys but lytyll Cotteswolld woll at Calleȝ, and y
understond Lombardys has bowght ytt up yn Ynglond,
and ȝe undyrstonde what sobstons is at London to schyppe.[1]
I hope ther whas nott a better markett toward for Cottes
woll many a day. I woll nott avysse ȝe to schype in the
dede [2] of wynter, ytt yss long lyyng,[3] fowlle whedyr, and
jepardes for stormys.

Of tydynges I con none wryght yow for sarten as ȝett,
but at myn howllde lady [4] ys comyng from Byng [5] to Sent
Tomers,[6] and the ambassetters bothe of Ynglond and
Fraunsse. Y connott say what whorlld whe shall have;
some of the Deukes Counsell wholld hawe whar, and
some pesse. The very grounde [7] must come howght of
Yngland. . . .

I woll that y myght undyrstond be wryttyng wher [8]
the kyng porposythe to hawe whar wᵗ Frawnsse or no . . .
yff y undyrstode be tymes, y myght, yff nede be, porvay
me of saffe condytt.[9] Y whollde forst ondyrstond how the
Kynge take my lordys answar, etc. No mor unto yow at
this tyme. . . .

per yowr son,

GEORGE CELY.

The Cely Papers.

[1] For shipping. [2] Dead.
[3] i.e. the wool would be lying too long aboard.
[4] Margaret, Dowager Duchess of Burgundy, sister to Edward IV.
[5] ? Buisgny or Binche. [6] St. Omer's. [7] The real cause?
[8] Whether. [9] Safe conduct.

From JOHN DALTON,

       To his brother-in-law, GEORGE CELY

Essex and London.   *22nd Sept.* 1481.

Right worchipfull Syr and Broder, after all dew recommendacyon hayd, I recomaund me unto you, and unto my Broder and yours, Rychard Cely. Further more, Syr, plese yow to wit that here hese be [1] Gysbreth van Wynbarow,[2] and I have sold hym the vj sarplers [3] of the Cottes old wooll . . . and as for fells,[4] I can seell non, ytte [5] God knowes I wold be ryght glayd to do that that myght be plesur unto you in sayelles or oder wayes, and yf ony Holonders come done,[6] I schall do my best in sayelles to my otterst poyer,[7] boyth in wooll and ych [8] feelles. I remember well that yow desered to my best [9] for Wylliam Maryon felles, and Syr, ytt schall nott be so forgetten, and Gud [10] wyll. . . . Syr, they laytter [11] end of next weke I purpose in to Flaunders. Alsoy,[12] Syr, I have wretten you affor thys that I have sent yow yowr gounysse,[13] the wych I trost ʒe have resevyd or thys tyme. Alsoy, Syr, your horson [14] doyth weell, God sawe [15] them; and, Syr, thys weke have we hayd in iij loodes heey [16] for you. . . .

Syr, I pray yow that I may be recomaundyd unto my mayster, your fayder, and moder. No more to yow at thys tyme, but our Lord send yow lang lyff and gud,[17] to His plesur and yours.

At Calley wᵗ owt gattes, the xxij day of September.

            Your Broder,

                JOHN DALTON.

                    The Cely Papers.

[1] Has been.   [2] Probably Guisbert van Winberg.
[3] Sacks.   [4] Whole skins, with the wool left on.
[5] Yet.   [6] Down.   [7] Uttermost power.   [8] Also.
[9] (me) to (do) my best. [10] God. [11] The latter. [12] Also. [13] Gowns.
[14] Horses (old wk. pl. inflexion).   [15] Save.   [16] Hay.   [17] Good.

F

From JOHN SKINNER,

To SIR WILLIAM STONOR

Modbury (Devon).   *17th Oct. c.* 1481.

Ry3th reverent and worcheppell Mayster, I recommende
me on to yowr Maysterchepp allso [1] hertely as I can and
may; prayeng yowr Maysterchepp to gete me a subpena [2]
for John Rowse apon þat he was ynfefyt yn treste [3] to
follfyll my fader ys wyll, and John Leghe and Water
Torryng, þe weche John Leghe and Water Torryng be
þe partyd [4] of þis worll, and so John Rowse is alyve, and y
deser he scholde folfyll my fader ys wyll. And yn þe
reverans of God, laboryd [5] ye to be scherve,[6] for hyt ys a
presentabell offise; þe worcheppefollyst yn þe scher [7]
have ben schervys, and yet theye hope to be: and Wylyam
Fowell sayde to me þat Syr Thomas Selynger hopyt to be
scherve þis yer: and Wylyam Fowell sayd hyt wer all so
convenyant and presentabell to yow as to hym, and sayd
hyt well [8] be worth to yow a C. nobelys abow [9] all costys,
and awayll mene hoder man [10] onder yow: and yef ye be
scherve I beseche yow that John Tollocke may be creyer [11]
of þe schere, and he shall plese yow also largely as heny
hoder schall, þe weche John Tollocke ys my soster sone.[12]
And I have send [13] on to yowr Maysterchepp for my wrethe [14]
of subpena by the berer of thys byll ii s. vj d.   And yet yn
þe reverens of God remembret [15] yowr sylve to labor to be
scherve . . . hyt ys beter to goveryn then to be goveryed
. . . I-wrethen at Modbere [16] on Synt Luke ys yeve.[17]

By your aune Syr John Schynner,

parson of Penyton.

The Stonor Letters and Papers.

[1] As.   [2] Subpoena.   [3] 'Enfeoffed in trust.'   [4] Departed.
[5] Labory*th* (imper. sg.).   [6] Sheriff.   [7] Shire.   [8] Will.
[9] Above.   [10] Avail many another man.   [11] Crier.   [12] My sister's son.
[13] Sent.   [14] Writ.   [15] Remembre*th* (imper. sg.).   [16] Modbury.   [17] Eve.

From RICHARD CELY, the Younger,

To his brother, GEORGE CELY

Essex and London. 5*th Nov.* 1481.

Riught whell belovid brother I recomend me wnto yow
wyth aull myne hart, informeyng yow at the makyng of
thys howr fathe and mother were whell comforttyd [1] and
sendys yow ther blessynges. Hyt whos so that,[2] be the
menys [3] of Brandon, howr father and I wher indyttyd for
scleyng of an hartte that whos drevyn into Kent, the
qweche whe [4] nevyr se ner knew of, and thys day I have
ben wt master Mwngewmtre,[5] and gevyn hym the whalew
of a pype whyn,[6] to have ws howt of the boke hevir hyt be
schewyd the Kyng,[7] and so he has promysyd me, and to be
good master to howr father and ws in the matter betwhene
Bra[n]ddon and hus. John Froste, Foster,[8] brohut me to hys
mastyrschyp and aqwaynttyd me wt a gentyll mane of hys,
hos name ys Ramston, that ys a ny mane [9] to master
Mongewmbre, and so I mwste informe hym my matters
at aull tymys, and he whyll sche [10] them to hys master. . .

I wndyrstonde that ȝe have a fayre hawke, I am ryught
glade of hyr, for I trwste to God sche schall make yow and
me ryught grehyt sport; ȝefe I whor sewyr [11] at what
passayge ȝe whollde send her, I whowlde fett hyr at Dowyr.
and kepe hyr tyll ȝe cwm. A grehyt inforttewin ys fawlyn
on yowr beche,[12] for sche had xiiij fayr whelpys and aftyr
that sche hade whelpyd, sche whelde newyr hett [13] mette,
and so sche ys deyd and aull her whelpys. . . .

[1] i.e. in good health; see OED. s.v. *Comfort*, sb. 6.
[2] It so happened that . . . [3] Means. [4] We.
[5] Sir Thomas Montgomery, Steward of the King's Forest of Essex.
[6] A pipe of wine. A pipe was a cask containing two hogsheads.
[7] Edward IV. [8] Forester.
[9] 'A near man,' one who has the confidence of.
[10] Show, reveal. [11] If I were sure. [12] Bitch. [13] Eat.

Jhesu kepe yow. Whr[y]tte at London, the **v** day of Nowembyr.

per yowr brother,

RYCHARD CELY.

The Cely Papers.

From *The Revelation to the Monk of Evesham,* 1196 [1]

c. 1482.

Thys man and prior y sawe and knew amonge the firste that were in peynys of the fyrste place of purgatorye that we came to. Trewly he was in ful grete and sore tormentys, and sofyrd ful greuys peynys, sym tyme in fyre and sum tyme in stinkyng bathys of brimston and pyche medild togedyr, hoys [2] face and chere was ouer wrechyd and dedful.[3] . . . And y enquyryd of hym whethir he so sofreyd so grete peynys for the fawtys the whiche he dyd in youthe . . . and he seyde, 'naye, . . . the couetyse ambycyon that y hadde to kepe my worschippe,[4] and the fere that y hadde to leue hit, so blyndyd the syghte of my soule that y lowsyd [5] the brydyl of correccyon to the willys of my sogettys [6] and sofryd hem to doo and folowe her desyrys and lustys as my yes [7] had be closyd, leste haply yef y had correcte [8] hem and refraynde hem from her lyghtnes, they wulle [9] haue be to me as enemyes to labure, and to haue me out of my worschippe. . . .' And all this y dyd a part [10] of myne owne lightnes, and a parte be cause y wolde defende

---

[1] The tale of a monk who visited Purgatory. First written in 1196, but the only extant version is this much later text printed by (?) William de Machlinia, *c.* 1482. See also Ralph of Coggeshall and Roger of Wendover, *sub anno,* 1196.

[2] Whose.   [3] So MS., perhaps for *dredful.*   [4] Office, dignity.
[5] Loosed.   [6] Subjects.   [7] As if my eyes.   [8] Corrected.
[9] Would. ME. *wyllen* (subj. imperf.).   [10] Partly.

my prelacyon.[1] And for hem to pleye lewde gamys and to speke and clathyr [2] tryfullys,[3] iapys [4] and other lewdnesse, and also to goo and wandyr amonge secler [5] folkys, and ydelnes, hyt was leful [6] to hem as hyt was to me . . . wherefore many of hem bode stylle in her fowle abusyons,[7] going fro euyll to wars.[8]

From *The Revelation to the Monk of Evesham,* 1196

c. 1482.

Trewly thawgh [9] y refusyd as mekyll as y myghte to see and beholde tho thinghes that were done yn that place,[10] y cowde not auoide the knoweleg of on clerk, the wyche y sawe and knew sum tyme. Thys clerk in hys days was a doctur of lawe and . . . was largely posseste with beneficys and rentys of the chirche, and . . . dayly he coueytyd to haue more and more, wherefore by the wille of god . . . he felle yn to grete sekenes. . . . Than the heuynly leche,[11] our sauyur, seyng that he was neuer in his dayes the bettyr for the sekenesse, the whiche he hadde for his warnyng, the whyche he schoyd [12] and gaue vnto hym for a gostely medeson, nethir wente owte of hys onclene leuing, in the whiche vnclene leuing he was in by the afflicyon of hys grete sekenesse: Therefore the euyll and wekid faites [13] and dedys that cowde not be clensyd and purged in hys yonge aage, oure lord Ihesu Crist mercefully putte and ende of hem in hys dethe. . . .

Thys forseyde clarke, the wyche y knew sum tyme in my chyldhode and yong aage, y vndyrstode nor y knewe

---

[1] Prelacy, office.   [2] Clatter.   [3] Trifles.   [4] Jests.   [5] Secular.
[6] Lawful.   [7] Here=sins.   [8] Worse.   [9] Though.
[10] i.e. purgatory.   [11] Leech, doctor.   [12] Showed.
[13] Evil deeds (OF. *fait.* Lat. *factum*).

not that he was dysceste [1] and ded. . . . Neuertelesse yn alle suche peynys and tormentys as hit ys aboue seyd y sawe and fownde hym, and y merueyled of hit. For y had wente [2] he had be yet a lyue and also an honest person.

From *The Archives of the Corporation of the City of London.*

Extracts from the Regulations of the Craft of Brewers.

London.   5*th Dec.* 1482.

Ffirst that every persone occupiyng the craft or feet [3] of bruyng within the ffraunchese of the said Citee, make or do to be made goode and hable ale and holesome for mannys body, convenable and accordyng in strength and fynesse to the price of the malt for the tyme being, and that no maner ale, after it be clensed and sett on jeyst,[4] be put to sale nor born oute to any custumers hous till that it have fully spourged,[5] and also be tasted and aviwed [6] by the Wardeyns of the said Craft. . . .

Also, that no maner persone occupiyng the said occupacion . . . take, receive or kepe in his house any mo apprentises at ones . . . than ii or iii at the moste, such as shalbe necessary unto hym and as he may honestly guyde and sett awerk in his owne service. And that every suche apprentice or [7] he be bounde or sett awerk . . . be presented by his maister, to the Wardeyns . . . in the comon hall of the said craft there openly to be seen and examyned of and uppon their birthe and clenesse of their bodies, and othere certeyn poyntes for the wirship [8] of the said Citee, and honeste of the ffeolaship of the said Craft of bruers. . . .

---

[1] Deceased.   [2] 'Had weened,' had supposed.

[3] i.e. feat, skill, trade.

[4] On joist, i.e. on a bench, or baulk of timber, to stand.

[5] Fermented.   [6] Inspected.   [7] Ere.   [8] Honour.

From RICHARD CELY, the Younger,

To his brother, GEORGE CELY

Essex and London. 13*th May* 1482.

Ruight interly whelbelovyd brothe, I recomende me
harttely unto yow. . . . Syr, I whryte to yow a prosses I
pray God send ther of a good heynd.[1] The same day that
I come to Norlache,[2] on a Sonday befor mattens from
[B]urforde, Wylliam Mydwyntter wyllecwmyd me, and in
howr comynycacyon [3] he askyd me hefe [4] I wher in any
whay of maryayge. I towlde hym, nay, and he informeyd
me that ther whos a ȝeunge gentyllwhoman, hos father
ys [5] name ys Lemryke, and her mother ys deyd, an sche
schaull dispend be her moter xl[ll] a ȝe,[6] as thay say in that
contre; and her father ys the gretteste rewlar as [7] rycheste
man in that contre, and ther hawhe [8] bene grete genttyll-
men to seyr,[9] and wholde hawhe her. And hewyr [10] matens
wher done, Wylliam Mydwynter had mevyd thys mater to
the gretteste mane a bot [11] the gentylman Lemeryke, and
he ȝeyd [12] and informyd the forsayd of aull the matter, and
the ȝewng gentyllwoman bothe . . . and the same mane
sayd to me, hefe I whowllde tary May day I schulde hawhe
a syte of the ȝeunge gentyllwhoman, and I sayd I wholld
tary w[t] a good wyll. . . .

And to mattens the same day come the ȝewnge gentyll
whoman and her mother i law, and I and Wylliam Bretten
wher seyng mattens when thay com in to chyrche; and
when mattens whos done thay whente to a kynnys whoman[13]

---

[1] I write to you of a matter, to which I pray God will give a good
conclusion.
[2] Northleach. [3] Conversation. [4] If. [5] Whose father's.
[6] A year. [7] So MS., perhaps for *and*. [8] Have.
[9] See her. [10] And befóre. [11] About, near.
[12] Yede, went. [13] Kinswoman.

of the ȝewnge gentty woman, and I sent to them a pottell
of whyte romnay,[1] and they toke hyt thankefully, for thay
had cwm a myle a fote that monyng [2]; and when mes [3]
whos done I come and whellcwmyd them, and kyssyd them;
and they thankyd me for the whyne and prayd me to cwm
to dyner w^t them . . . and the person [4] plesetheyde me
whell, as be [5] the fyrste comenycacyon sche is ȝewnge,
lytyll,[6] and whery [7] whellfavyrd, and whytty [8]; . . .
Syr, aull thys matter abydythe the cwmyng of her father
to London, that whe may wndyrstonde what some [9] he
wyll departe w^t, and how he lykys me.　He wyll be heyr [10]
w^{t}in iij whekes.　I pray send me a letter how ȝe thynke
be thys matter. . . .

The Cely Papers.

From Sir John Weston, Prior of St. John's,

To his cousin, George Cely

Essex. 　　　　　　　　　　　　　　　*27th Oct.* 1487.

Worshipfull Coyssyn, wyt du recomendassions premysit,[11]
it is so I come [12] to Rome the xv day of Octobre, and was
ryt welcome. . . . The pope hollynes made me gret cher,
and wallde a [13] sente me home agayn, and follet [14] me of al
mannor abedyensses or comandementt made to me or
motte be made; [15] bot I, Syr, desyret [16] is hollynes at [17] I
mette [18] do my vayage,[19] sennes I was so far fourthe, and so
is ollyness sendes me as is imbassador wyt materis of gret
importannss.　I truste do [20] be the sonner [21] a come by

[1] Romney.　　　　　[2] Morning.　　　[3] Mass.
[4] i.e. the young woman.　　　[5] By.　　[6] Short, small.
[7] Very.　　[8] Intelligent.　　[9] Sum, i.e. as dowry.　　[10] Here.
[11] Premised.　[12] Came.　[13] Would have.　[14] Released, excused.
[15] Might be made.　　　　[16] Desired.　　　　[17] That.
[18] Might.　　　[19] Voyage.　　　[20] To.　　　[21] Sooner.

Godes grace. Coyssyn, as toshith [1] the mater of the staple, Ryscharde Herȝon, the kynges proctor, and I as don in that mater as meche as motte be don to fulfylle the kynges intente, and the wel [2] of the marchantes of the staple; for I take God to recorde, and the brynger of this gere, at [3] I dede in is [4] as mess [5] as I wolde affe don ånd they ad gyn [6] me a gret gud [7] . . .

Coyssyn, I pray ȝow sende me worde of your welfare, and comande [8] me to my fader and ȝours, and your moder, and Jhesu keppe yow. At Rome the xxvij day of October, 1487.

Be your coyssyn, Syr John Weston,
PRYOR OF SANTJOHNS.

The Cely Papers.

From *The Greyfriars' Chronicle* [9]

London.   *c.* 1494.

1407. Thys yere one Travers a yoman of the crowne of the kynges, was hongyd at Tyborne for powsenynge [10] of hys wyffe and one Pylle in the counter in the Powltre. [11] And this yere alle the kydelles and trungkes [12] thorowgh-out the Temse from the towne of Stanes [13] in the west unto the watter of Medevey [14] in the est, by the mayer and commonalte of London were dystrowyd [15] and brent, and

---

[1] As toucheth, as regards.   [2] Weal, good.   [3] That.
[4] This.   [5] *Meche*, much.   [6] Given.
[7] Good, reward.   [8] Commend.
[9] Originally part of the Register in Greyfriars Monastery, London.
[10] Poisoning.
[11] At the court of justice in the Poultry (see OED., s.v. *Counter*, sb. 3, iii 6).
[12] Perforated floating boxes, in which little fish are kept.
[13] Staines.   [14] Medway.   [15] Destroyed.

gret plee [1] and dyscorde was for that matter betwene Thomas Arundelle, archebyshoppe of Canterbery and other lorddes and knyghtes on that one party,[2] and the mayor and commonalte of London on that other party. . . . And thys yere was furst ordened a masse of the Holy Gost to be songe solemply be note every yere at the Yeldehalle chappelle the same daye the mayer is chosyn.

1411. Thys yere was ordened the alay [3] of golde. . . . And this yere was the grete frost and ise and the most sharpest wenter that ever man sawe, and it duryd fourteen wekes, so that men myght in dyvers places both goo and ryde over the Temse.

1414. Thys yere the kynge wanne [4] Harflew in Normandy. And this yere Richard Gurmon, French baker of Lumberstreth,[5] was brent in Smythfelde. . . . And the v daye of August nexte ware [6] put to deth at Hamton,[7] Sir Richard of Yorke, erle of Chambrych,[8] the lorde Scroppe,[9] and sir Thomas Grey knyght, for treson, imagenynge [10] the kynges deth. . . . And the morrow after sent Laurens day the kynge with hys pepulle sheppyd at Porchemowth.[11] . . .

From Margaret, Queen of Scotland,[12]

To her father, King Henry VII

London.   1503–4.

My moste dere lorde and fader, in the most humble wyse that I can thynke I recummaund me unto your Grace, besechyng you off your dayly blessyng, and that it will

---

[1] Debate.   [2] On the one side.   [3] Alloy.
[4] Won.   [5] Lombard Street.   [6] Were.   [7] Hampton, Southampton.
[8] Cambridge.   [9] Scrope.   [10] Plotting.   [11] Portsmouth.
[12] Married James IV of Scotland in 1503, when she was in her thirteenth year.

please you to yeve hartely thankes to all your servauntts the whych be your commaundement have geven ryght good attendaunce on me at this time, and specially to all thes ladies and jantilwomen which hath accompeneyed me hydder, and to geff credence to thys good lady the berar her off for I have showde hyr mor off my mynd than I will wryght at thys tyme. . . .

Sir, as for newys, I have none to send but that my lorde of Surrey ys yn great favor with the Kyng her that he cannott forber the companey off hym no tyme off the day. He and the bichopp off Murrey orderth every thyng as nyght [1] as they can to the Kyngs pleasur. I pray God it may be for my por hartts ease in tyme to come. They calnot [2] my Chamberlayne to them, whych [3] I am sur wull speke better for my part than any off them that ben off that consell. And iff he speke any thyng for my cause my lord of Surrey hath such wordds unto hym that he dar speke no furder. God send me comford to hys pleasur, and that I and myne that ben lefftt her with me be well entretid such wayse as they have taken. [4] For Godes sak Syr oulde [5] mea escwysd that I wryt not my sylf to your Grace, for I han no layfyr [6] thys tym, bot wyt a wishse I would I wer wyt your Grace now, and many tyms mor wan I wold andsyr. As for thys that I have wrytyn to your Grace, yt ys wery tru, bot I pray God I may fynd yt wel for my welef erefter.[7] No more to your Grace at thys tym, bot our Lord han you en ys kepyng. Wrytyn wyt the hand of your humble douter.

MARGARET.

Ellis's 'Original Letters.'

[1] Nigh.   [2] Call not.   [3] Who.
[4] Margaret writes from here to the end herself.   [5] Hold.
[6] So Ellis—read *laysyr*.   [7] Welfare (here)after.

From GEORGE TREVELYAN,[1]

To his brother, SIR JOHN TREVELYAN.

Cornwall.   *27th Jan. c.* 1503.

Ryght Worschypfull Brother, yn my most hartte maner
I recomaund me unto you. Syr, as for your standerde
[2] wylle coste you xxvj s. viij d. bysydds youre sylke and
frange [3] for hyt, and I have promyste Garthere [4] for hys
labure a nage.[5] I wylle, God ys grace sone apone candelmas
by [6] w^t you and bryng your standerde.

My lorde marques [7] hath send unto my lorde bosschope
of Exeter a letter for confermyng ye benefysse [8] of lawe.
I have wryte unto Mr. Dene of Exeter a letter, and ye copy
off my Lord Bysschyp ys letter w^t yn hys letter. Ye may
looke apone ye letterys that ys send to Master Dene, and
ther ye schall see all ye novells [9] of ye Corte. Y wolde [10]
wrytyne them yn youre letter, but ye may see them yn
Mr. Dene ys letter, and alsoo my cosyne wolle schowe them
you by moth [11] and other more. . . .

The armys off Carminow,[12] Garter seth, y^t [13] sholde be
gevyne w^t a labell of iij poyntts gulls,[14] came of the iij
brotherys. When ye ware made knytt ther wher but iiij
cottes off recorde yn Garterys booke, ye wyche I have send
you as y^t was put yn Garterys boke of atoryte.[15] As for
ye tother iiij coteys he wylle not put them yn hys boke tylle
he know your progeny lynyally, from hensse [16] they cum and

[1] One of Henry VIII's chaplains, and rector of Mawgan-in-the-
menage, Kerrier (Cornwall).
    [2] Supply, 'it.'   [3] Fringe.   [4] Garter King of Arms.
    [5] Nag.   [6] Be.   [7] The Marquis of Dorset.
    [8] i.e. his rectorship of Mawgan.   [9] News.
    [10] Supply 'have.'   [11] Mouth.
    [12] Sir J. Trevelyan was, by virtue of the marriage of one of his an-
cestors, to quarter the arms of Carminow.   [13] That.
    [14] Gules.   [15] Authority.   [16] Whence.

by home [1] you bere them. He marlys [2] that he founde not them yn hys fatherys boke of atoryte as ye other armys ware. . . . yf any mane cum schorte [3] to London send ye uppe money . . . for at ye makyne [4] of this letter y had not aboffe v s. yn my porsse,[5] as knowythe God, hoo send you good lyffe and long. Frome Grenewych ye xxvijth day of Januarye.

Youre brother,

GEORGE TREVELYAN.

The Trevelyan Papers.

From WILLIAM BURBANK [6]

To KING HENRY VIII

London.   *28th Aug.* 1514.

Pleas it your most excellent Grace to witt that, as touchyng the cause [of the] deithe of my Lorde and Master, my Lorde Cardinall, your Graces late Orator, because that aswell affore his departor by the Phisecians as aftur by a . . . man that oppynyd his body by the Popis commandmentt, itt was juged . . . he shuld have been posonyd,[7] or att the leste grett tokens and as some . . . saide manyfest thyngs therof apperide, the Popes said holines haith sith [8] caused moste diligentt and exactt examynacion to be maide uppon the same. And by cause that it was known all most manyfestlie that the busshop of Worcestr, now y^r Graces Orator, was enymye unto my said Lorde, itt was sodenlie noiside throughe the citie that he shulde have

---

[1] Whom.   [2] Marvels.   [3] Shortly, soon [OE. *sceorte* (adv.)]
[4] Making.   [5] Purse.

[6] Secretary (according to Pollard, steward) to Cardinal Baynbrigge (Bainbridge), who was sent on an embassy to Pope Julius II by Henry VIII in 1511.   [7] Poisoned.   [8] Since.

[been] auctor of this great pretendid [1] offence. A certan prest namyd Ranalde [of] Modena [2] was moche in my lords chamber and alway dere and fa[miliar] with the said busshop of Worcestr. . . . The said Ranalde . . . haith oppenlie confesside that he hym self putt poson into my said lords potage att the desire and conduction [3] thereunto of the busshop of Worcestr. . . . He saith he did by [4] the said poson in a Citie namyd Sp[oleto] nott verray farr from Rome, and kepid itt a good space in his chambre under a tyyll [5] stoon. All this his confession is writen in the proctor his booke by his own hande *in processu*. And sithen the said Ranalde [hath] written this his confession [in] his awne hande. . . . Nott oonlie the said Ranalde haith thus confesside and writen the same of his own hande, butt also confermyd itt with oon grett oithe.[6] . . . Uppon the morow aftur the said Ranalde, with a small knyff that he had secrett smott hym self, wolfully [7] intending to have killed hym self, and thereof is in poontt [8] of deithe as is supposide without recovery; and saith that he knowth perfitelie to be perpetually for this act dampnyd. . . . Som ther be that haith noside [9] in Rome how that the poson shuld have been sentt from England by som prelate thare, being enemye unto my said late Lorde, and procuride the same to be mynystrid unto hym by his cooke. Where-uppon soundrie men hath inquyred the same boith [10] of my said felo [11] and me, whereunto we aunswerde that our master had no such enymyes in England, ne that Prelates of Englande and English borne wer ever disposed unto ony suche actes. . . .

---

[1] Supposed, alledged.   [2] Rinaldo de Modena.   [3] Instigation.
[4] Buy.   [5] Tile.   [6] Oath.
[7] Wilfully.   [8] Point.   [9] Noised.
[10] Both.   [11] Richard Pace, a fellow secretary.

Thus I shall duryng lyve humble bisiche our Lorde Jhū
for the preservation of your Graces most hygh and roiall
astate. From Florence the xxviij[th] day of Auguste,
M.D.xiiij.

> Your Graces most lawlie [1]
>> faithfull and trewe subgett
>>> [WILLIAM BURBANK].
>>>> *Ellis's 'Original Letters '*

From MARY, QUEEN OF FRANCE,[2]
> To her brother, KING HENRY VIII
>> *9th Sept.* 1515.

My most derest and ryt entierly belowyde Lord and
brothare, yn my most humble wys I recommande me unto
yowr Grace, shawynge [3] unto yowr Grace that I do a pa . . .
by my Lord my howsbande [4] that y[ou] ar playsayde and
contentyde that he shale resorde [5] on to yowr presence at
swche tyme as yowr Grace shale be at hys maner of Donyng-
ton, wherby I se wele he hys merwosly [6] rejoysyd and moche
comfortyd that yt hathe lyked yowr Grace so to be play-
sayd; for the wyche yowr specyale goodnys to hym showyd
yn that be halfe, and for sondry and many oder yowr
kyndnes, as wele to me as to hym showed and gewyn yn
dyvers cawsys, I most humbly thanke yowr Grace; assew-
ryng yow that for the same I accompt myself as moche
bonden un to yowr Grace as ewer swster was to brother;

[1] Lowly.

[2] Married Louis XII, 5th November, 1514. Louis died in the
following January.

[3] Showing.

[4] Mary, after Louis's death, married Charles Brandon, Duke of
Suffolk.

[5] Resort. [6] Marvellously.

and accordyng ther un to I shale to the beste of my powr dowryng my lyef end[e]ver myselfe as ferre as in me shale be possyble to do the thyng that shale stond with yowr playsowr, and yf it had be tyme convenyente to yowr Grace hade be ther wythe pleasyd I wolde most gladly have accompanyd my sayd Lord yn thys yowrnay.[1] Bwt I trowst that bowthe I and my sayd Lord shal se yow acordyng as yowr Grace worte [2] yn yowr laste Letters unto my sayde Lorde, wych ys the thyng that I dessyr more to opteyn [3] than all the honor off the Worlde. . . .

From Letheryng in Swf.[4] the ix day off Septembur by the hand of yowr lowyng suster,

MARY QUENE OFF FRANCE.

Ellis's 'Original Letters.'

From Sir Richard Torkington's [5] *Pilgrimage*

Mulbarton (Norfolk).   *March 1517 to April 1518.*

Thursday the ij[de] Day of Julii a bowt xj or xij of the Cloke a for non we com to Candi, itt is callyd otherwyse Crete, ther be ryht Ill Peple, it is vnder the Venyschyans.[6] Ther we ffonde vj or vij englissh Marchaunts whiche [7] made vs good cher.   And they gaff to vs at our Dep[ar]tyng to the Shippe Muskedele as myche as fyllyd our botellys. . . .

In Candia ther growe grett Vynes, And specially of malwesy [8] and muskadell. . . .

In Candi Also ys the old Churche wherof Titus was Bysshoppe to whom Pole [9] wrott Epystyllis, I saw the hede

---

[1] Journey.   [2] Wrote.   [3] Obtain.   [4] Suffolk.

[5] Sir Richard was Rector of Mulbarton, being presented to the living in 1511 by Sir Thomas Boleyn, afterwards Earl of Wiltshire, and father of Anne Boleyn.

[6] Venetians.   [7] Who.   [8] Malvoisie.   [9] Paul.

of the seyd Titus Coverd w[t] sylver and golde, it ys ther excedyngly hoote . . . thys Ile ys a grett Ile and a Plenteows of all maner of thyngs. They be Grekes in that Ile And the Vencions ben Lord ther, And every yer or every other yer ys Chosyn a Duke by the same Venycions.

Ther groweth the Voyne [1] that ys callyd Malweysy and muskedell. . . .

In that londe xxx myle from Candy ys an old brokyn Citee whiche was callyd Cretina, And a lityll ther by syd stondyth an old Churche which was byldyd in the honor of Jhu Criste And holowyd [2] in the worshipe of Titus Epi*scopus* to whome Seynt Poule wrott in Actibus A*postolorum* Ad Titum. . . . And ther was grett hete, ffor from May to Halowmesse [3] ther groweth no gresse, It is so brent with the hete of the sone.

From Sir Richard Torkington's *Pilgrimage*

Mulbarton (Norfolk).   *March* 1517 *to April* 1518.

At Bethelem comonly be v or vj friers of Mowte Syon to kepe the holy place ther, whiche with other fryers that cam with us to Mownte Syon, Dressed them [4] to solempne procession at our fyrst commyng, whome we folowyd to all the holy placys with in the same Monasteri with candels light in ower handys as all wey vsyd in other place wher ony procession was Don.

And fyrst the seyd procession browght vs to a place at an Aulter in the suth yle wher our Savyr Crist was Circumsysed.

And from thens we came to an other Auter on the Northe

---

[1] Vine.   [2] Hallowed.
    [3] Hallowmas.   [4] Prepared themselves.

syd wher the iij kyngs made redy ther offeryngs to present on to ower Savor Criste.

And from thys place, Descendyng certayne grees [1] of stone we com in to a wonder fayer lityll Chapel at the hyer auter wherof ys the vary place of the byrth of our lord, Assigned by a sterre made in a fayer whith [2] marble stone, Vnder the myddys of the seyd high Auter whych byrth was Don in the self most holy place to the gretest Joy and gladnesse that ever cam to mankynde. . . . And ther by ys a lityll Auter sum what vnder the Rook [3] wher the iij kyngs offered to ower blyssyd Savyor Criste Jhu, Gold, Myrre and Incence. . . .

And vndowtyd thys lityll Chapell of the byrthe of ower lord ys the most glorius and Devowte place that ys in the world, Somyche thot [4] that excedith in holynesse all other places that be in this worlde.

It ys Also of tables [5] of fyne whith marble stone. And the vowtys [6] be garnyshyd with gold, and byse [7] with Diverse storys of a substyll musyk [8] werke as may be. The walles also of all the body of the Chirche from the pyllers to the Rooff be poyntyd [9] with storys from the begynnyng of the world of the same musyng [10] werkys, whyche ys the Richeest thyng that canne be Don to any wallis.

From *The Greyfriars' Chronicle*
London.   1529-31.

1529. This yere was a prisoner brake from the halle at Newgate whan the cecions was done, that was browte downe in a basket, and brake thorow the pepull and went unto

---

[1] Steps.   [2] White.   [3] Rock.   [4] That.
[5] Slabs.   [6] Vaults, i.e. arches and roofs.   [7] Beset.
[8] Skilful mosaic.   [9] Painted.   [10] Mosaic.

the Grayfreeres,[1] and there was vij dayes. And at the last
the shreffes [2] came and spoke with hym in the church, and,
for because he wolde not abjure and aske a crowner,[3] with
gret violens of them and their offecers toke him owte of the
churche, and soo the churche was shott [4] in from monday
unto thursday, and the servys and masse sayd and songe in
the fratter [5]; and that day the bushoppe of sent Asse [6]
browte the sacrament solemply downe with procession, and
soo the powre prisoner continewyd in prisone, for they sowte
all the wayes that they cowde, but the lawe wolde not serve
them to honge hym, and at the last was delyvered and put
at lyberte.[7]

Also this same yere, John Scotte, that was one of the
kynges playeres,[8] was put in Newgate for rebukynge of the
shreffes, and was there a sennet,[9] and at the last was ledde
betwene two of the offecers from Newgate thorrow London,
and soe to Newgat agayne, and then was delyveryd home
to hys howse, but he toke soch a thowte [10] that he dyde, for
he went in hys shurte.

1531. And this yere was gret wyndes and fluddes that
dyde moch harme both a [11] thys syde the see and beyende
the see.

From CARDINAL WOLSEY,
To DR. STEPHEN GARDINER [12]

London.   *c.* 1530.

My owne goode mastyr Secretary aftyr my moste herty
commendacons I pray you at the reverens of God to help

---

[1] i.e. into sanctuary.   [2] Sheriffs.   [3] Coroner.   [4] Shut.
[5] Fratry.   [6] St. Asaph (i.e. Henry Standish).   [7] Liberty.
[8] i.e. an actor in the King's Company.
[9] i.e. a seven-night, week.
[10] Gave way to such great grief, became so melancholy, grieved.
[11] On.   [12] Afterwards Bishop of Winchester.

that exspedicion be usyd in my presents,[1] the delay wherof
so replenyssheth my herte with hevynes that I can take no
reste; nat for any vayne fere but onely for the miserabli
condycion that I am presently yn, and lyclyhod to contynue
in the same onles that ye in whom ys myn assuryd truste,
do helpe and releve me therein; for fyrst contynuyug here
in thys moweste [2] and corrupt eyer beyng enteryd in to the
passyon of the dropsy, *cum prost[r]atione appetitus et continuo
insompnus,* I cannat lyve; wherfor of necessyte I muste be
removyd to summe other dryer eyer and place, wher I may
have comodyte of Physycyans. Secondly havynge but
Yorke wych ys now decayd by viijC.li. by the yeere, I can
nat tell how to lyve and kepe the poore nombyr of folks
wych I nowe have. . . . Remembyr, good Mr. Secretary,
my poore degre and what servys I have done: and howe
nowe approchyng to deth I must begyn the world ageyn.
I beseeche yow therfor, movyd with pity and compassyon,
soker me in thys my calamyti, and to your power, wych I
do knowe ys gret, releve me. . . . And as my poore [3] shall
increase so I shall not fayle to acquyte yo[r] kyndnes. Wryt-
tyn hastely at Asher [4] with the rude and shackyng hand of
your dayly bedysman and assuryd frende.

T. Car[lis] Ebor.

Ellis's ' Original Letters.'

From Sir Thomas Elyot's *The Boke Named the Gouernour
Wiltshire and London.*   1531.

If the childe be of nature inclined, (as many have ben),
to paint with a penne, or to fourme images in stone or
tree: he shulde nat be therfrom withdrawen, or nature be

---

[1] Affairs.   [2] Moist.   [3] Power.   [4] Esher.

rebuked, whiche is to hym beniuolent: but puttyng one to him, whiche is in that crafte, wherein he deliteth, moste excellent, in vacant tymes from other more serious lernynge, he shulde be in the moste pure wise enstructed in painting or keruinge.[1]

And nowe, perchance, some enuious reder wyll hereof apprehende occasion [2] to scorne me, sayenge that I haue well hyed [3] me to make of a noble man a mason or peynter. And . . . yet . . . what pleasure and also utilitie is it to a man whiche intendeth to edifie, hymselfe to expresse the figure of the warke [4] that he purposeth, accordyng as he hath conceyued it in his owne fantasie? . . . More ouer the feate of portraiture [5] shall be an allectiue [6] to euery other studie or exercise. . . . Finally euery thinge that portrature may comprehende will be to him delectable to rede or here.   And where the liuely spirite, and that whiche is called the grace of the thyng, is perfectly expressed, that thinge more persuadeth and stereth [7] the beholder, and soner istructeth hym than the declaration in writynge or speak-ynge doth the reder or hearer.   Experience we haue therof in lernynge of geometry, astronomie and cosmogrophie, called in englisshe the discription of the world.   In which studies I dare affirme a man shal more profite in one wike [8] by figures and chartis . . . than he shall by the only reding or heryng the rules of that science by the space of halfe a yere at the lest; wherefore the late writers deserue no small commendation whiche added to the autors [9] of those sciences apt and propre figures.[10]

[1] Sculpture.   [2] Seize an opportunity.
[3] Hied.   [4] Work.   [5] Art of painting.
[6] Inducement.   [7] Stirreth.   [8] Week.
[9] Authors.   [10] Diagrams, illustrations.

From Sir Thomas Elyot's *The Boke Named the Gouernour*
Wiltshire and London.   1531.

. . . how farre out of reason shall we iudge them to be
that wolde exterminate all superioritie, extincte [1] all
gouernaunce and lawes, and under the coloure of holy
scripture, whiche they do violently wraste [2] to their purpose,
do endeuour them selfes to bryng the life of man into a
confusion ineuitable, and to be in moche wars [3] astate than
the afore named beestes?   Sens [4] without gouernaunce
and lawes the persones moste stronge in body shulde by
violence constraigne them that be of lasse [5] strength and
weaker to labour as bondemen or slaues for their sustin-
aunce and other necessaries, the stronge men beinge without
labour or care; Than [6] were all our equalitie dasshed, and
finally as bestes sauage the one shall desire to slee a nother.
I omitte continuall manslaughters, rauisshementes, aduou-
tries [7] and enormities horrible to reherce, whiche, (gouernaunce lackynge) muste nedes of necessitie ensue, except [8]
these euangelicall persones coulde perswade god, or com-
pelle him to chaunge men into aungels, makinge them all
of one disposition, and confirminge them all in one fourme
of charitie.   And as concerninge all men in a generaltie,
this sentence, 'knowe thy selfe,' whiche of all other is
moste compendious, beinge made but of thre wordes, euery
worde beinge but one sillable, induceth men sufficiently
to the knowlege of iustyce.

From *The Greyfriars' Chronicle*
London.   1538–46.

1538. And the furst sonday of September was hongyd
at Clarkenwell at the wrestlynge place the hongman that

[1] Extinguish, do away with.   [2] Wrest.   [3] Worse.   [4] Since.
            [5] Less.   [6] Then.   [7] Adulteries.   [8] Unless.

was before, and ij with him, for stelynge in Bartylmew fayer.[1]

1540. . . . this . . . yere, the xvj day of March was one Gomer and iij vacabundes [2] with him draune, hongyd and qwarterd for cleppynge of golde, at Tyborne.

1546. . . . the xiij day of June after was Wytsonsonday, and then was a generalle processione from Powlles un to sent Peters in Cornehylle, with alle the chelderne of Powlles scole, and a crosse of every parishe churche, . . . alle the clarkes, alle the presttes, with parsons and vekeres [3] of every church in coppys,[4] and the qwere [5] of Powlles in the same maner, and the byshoppe bereynge the sacrament under a canapy, with the mayr in a gowne of cremsone velvet, the aldermen in scarlet, with alle the crafttes in their best aparelle; and whan the mayer came betwene the crosse and the standert [6] there was made a proclamacyon with dyvers harhoddes [7] of armes and pursevanttes [8] in their cote armeres,[9] with the trompettes, and ther was proclamyd a unyversalle pes for ever betwene the emparar,[10] the kynge of Ynglonde,[11] the French kynge,[12] and alle crystyne kynges for ever.

From THE PRINCESS ELIZABETH,

　　To her brother, KING EDWARD VI, with a present
　　of her portrait

London. 1540–50.

Like as the richeman that dayly gathereth riches to riches and to one bag of mony layeth a greate sort til it

---

[1] Bartholomew Fair.	[2] Vagabonds.	[3] Vicars.
[4] Copes.	[5] Choir.	[6] Standard.
[7] Heralds.	[8] Pursuivants.	[9] Coat-armour.
[10] Charles V.	[11] Henry VIII.	[12] Francis I.

come to infinit, so methinkes your Maiestie, not beinge suffised withe many benefits and gentilnes [1] shewed to me afore this time, dothe now increase them in askinge and desiring wher you may bid and commaunde, requiring a thinge not worthy the desiringe for it selfe, but made worthy for your Higthnes request.   My pictur I mene, in wiche if the inward good mynde towarde your grace migth as well be declared as the outwarde face and countenaunce shal be seen, I wold nor haue taried the commandement but preuent [2] it, nor have bine the last to graunt but the first to offer it.   For the face, I graunt I might wel blusche to offer, but the mynde I shal neuer be ashamed to present. For thogth [3] from the grace of the pictur the coulers may fade by time, may giue by wether, may be spotted by chaunce; yet the other nor time with her swift winges shal ouertake nor the mistie cloudes with ther loweringes may darken, nor chance with her slipery fote may ouerthrow. Of this, althogth yet the profe coulde not be great bicause the occasions hathe bine smal, notwithstandinge as a dog hathe a daye, so may I perchaunce have time to declare it in dides [4] wher now I do write them but in wordes.   And further I shal most humbly beseche your Maiestie that whan you shal loke on my pictur you wil witsafe [5] to thinke that as you haue but the outwarde shadow of the body afore you, so my inwarde minde wischeth that the body it selfe wer oftner in your presence. . . .

From Hatfilde [6] this 15 day of May.

Your Maiesties most humbly sistar,

ELIZABETH.

Ellis's 'Original Letters.'

[1] Plural.	[2] Anticipated.	[3] Though.
[4] Deeds.	[5] Vouchsafe.	[6] Hatfield.

From *The Greyfriars' Chronicle*

London.   1549–50.

1549. . . . in this yere moche pepulle of the comyns dyd ryse in divers places in the realme, and pullyd downe parkes and growndes that was inclosyd of dyvers lordes and gentylmen within the realme from the powre men.

Item, the xxvij day of June there was sent a commande-ment from the councelle unto Powlles that they shulde have no more the Apostylles masse in the mornynge, nor our Lady masse, nor no communyone at no aultelle [1] in the church but at the hye awlter. . . . Item, on Bartyl-mew evyne was shott dyvers goonnes at the gattes in London. . . .

Item, the last day of the . . . monyth the byshoppe of Cauntorbery [2] shulde a come agayne to Powlles, and a preched agayne, but he send Josephe [3] hys chaplyne, and he preched in the qwere of the subdewynge of them that dyd rysse . . . and how [4] mysery they ware browte unto, and there he rehersyd as hys master dyd before that the occasyone came by popysse presttes. . . . Item, this same day Cardmaker [5] sayd opynly in hys lector in Powlles that if God ware a man he was a vj or vij foote of lengthe, with the bredth,[6] and if it be soo, how canne it be that he shuld be in a pesse of brede in a rownde cake on the awter: what an ironyos [7] oppynyone is this unto the leye pepulle!

This yere, the vj day of December was Bodylys wyffe, the smythes w[yffe at Long lane] ende in Smythfelde hongyd at Tyborne for the dystrowynge of [her chil]derne. . .

---

[1] Side-altar.   [2] Thomas Cranmer.
[3] John Joseph, S.T.P.   [4] i.e. what.
[5] John Cardmaker, Vicar of St. Bride's, burnt 1555.   He read in St. Paul's three times a week.
[6] i.e. with the proportionate breadth.   [7] Erroneous.

1550. Item, that there came a sheppe [1] of egges and shurttes [2] and smockes owte of France to Byllynges gatte. . . Item, this yere . . . one man felle doune in Powlles church and brake hys necke for kecheynge [3] of pegyns in the nyght the iiij day of December.

From *The Greyfrairs' Chronicle*
London.   1551–6.

1551. And the xxvij day of the same monyth [i.e. June], the byshoppe of Wynchester, that was than [John Ponet], was devorsyd from hys wyffe in Powlles, the whyche was a bucheres wyff of Nottynggam, and gave hare husbande a sartyne mony a yere dureynge hys lyffe as it was jugydde by the lawe. . . .

Item, the xiij day of January was whyppyd vij women at the carttes arse, iiij at one [4] and iij at another, for vacobondes that wold not labor, but play the unthryftes. . . .

Item, the xxvj day of [Februarij,] the wyche was fryday, was hongyd at Towre hylle, sir Myllys Partyge [5] knyght, the wych playd wyth kynge Henry the VIII[te] at dysse [6] for the grett belfery that stode in Powlles church-yerde. . . .

1552. . . . the xxv day of October was the pluckynge downe of alle the alteres and chappelles in alle Powlles churche, with alle the toumes, at the commandment of the byshoppe, then beynge Nicolas Rydley, and alle the goodly stoneworke that stode behynde the hye alter . . . and wolde a pullyd downe John a Gauntes tome but there was a commandment [to] the contrary. . . .

1553. The v of August at vij a clocke at nyght came home Edmond Boner, byshoppe [from the Ma]rchelse [7] lyke a

---

[1] Ship.   [2] Shirts.   [3] Catching.
[4] i.e. at one time.   [5] Sir Miles Partridge.   [6] Dice.
[7] He had been imprisoned in the Marshalsea.

byshoppe, that alle the pepulle by the way badde hym welcom home, man and woman, and as many of the women as myghte kyssyd hym, and soo came to Powlles. . . .

1556. . . . the xviij day of August the mayer dynned at the rederes denner [1] at the Tempulle, and at after-none whane he was goynge, the swerde was willed to be borne doune in the closter,[2] but the sword-berer woold not.

From Henry Machyn's *Diary* [3]

London.   *June–July* 1552.

The xvij of Juin ther wher sett on the pelore [a man and] a woman; the woman boythe [4] a pesse of mottun [and when she] had ytt, she toke a pesse of a tylle [5] and frust [6] yt [into the] myds of the mottun, and she sayd that she had ytt of b[utcher, and would ha]ve ym punnyssyd; for ytt was hangyd over the pelore, and so there wher they sett boythe.[7] . . .

The furst day of July ther was a man and a woman on the pelere in Chepe-syd; the man sold potts of straberries, the whyche the pott was nott alff fulle, but fyllyd with forne; the man nam ys Grege; sum-tyme he con[terfeited] ym selffe a profett, for he was taken for [it, and] sett by the pelere in Sowthwarke. . . .

The xv day of July was wypyd a yong man and ij women for vyssyones and synes; and the[n] she was putt on the pelorie, for she wold [have] poysenyd her husband, for the same woman [permitted] her servand to com in to here.

---

[1] Readers' dinner.   [2] Cloister.
[3] Machyn was a Funeral Upholder in London, and a member of the Merchant Taylors' Guild.
[4] Bought.   [5] Tile.   [6] Thrust.   [7] Both.

From Henry Machyn's *Diary*

London.   *June–July* 1554.

The xxix day of Juin, the wyche was sant Peter and Powlles day, was a fayre at Westmynster abbay; and ther was a goodly pressessyon, and after masse; and ther the prynse of Pymon [1] and dyvers Spaneards, and hard messe in kyng Henry the vij chapelle.

The vj day of Julij was a goodly sermon [by] on of the prebendares of Powlles; and ther was a nuw skaffold mayd ther for the mayd that spake in the wall and wystelyd in Althergat stret; and she sayd openly that yt was on John Drake, ser Antony Knevett servand; and she whept petefully, and she knelyd and askyd God mercy, and the quen; and bad all pepull be ware of false thechyng,[2] for she sayd that she shuld have many goodly thynges gyffyn her. . . .

The xxj day of July by x of the cloke [was proclaimed] thrug London that the prynche of Spayne [3] was [arrived at Southampton] and that evere pere and lord and lade shuld [resort] unto her grace [4] cete of Wynchester with all spede to her graceus weddyng.

From Henry Machyn's *Diary*

London.   *April* 1555.

The xiiij day of Aprell, the wyche was [Ester day,] at sant Margatt parryche at Westmynster, af[ter masse] was done, one of the menysters, a prest of the ab[bay,] dyd helpe hym that was the menyster [to] the pepull who wher reseyvyng of the blessyd sacrament of [the lord] Jhesus Cryst, ther cam in to the chyrche a man that was a monke

[1] Piedmont.   [2] Teaching.   [3] Philip II.   [4] Queen Mary.

of Elly, the wyche was marryed to a wyff; the sam day
ther that sam man sayd to the menyster, What doyst thow
gyff them? and as sone as he had spokyn he druw his
wod-knyffe, and hyt the prest on the hed and struck hym a
grett blowe, and after ran after hym and struck hym on the
hand, and cloyffe [1] ys hand a grett way, and after on the
harme a grett wond; and ther was syche a cry and showtt
as has not byne; and after he was taken and cared to
presun, and after examynyd wher-for he dyd ytt.

The xx day of Aprell [he] was raynyd [2] at Powlles a-for
the bysshope of London and many odur and my lord cheyffe
justys and my lord mayre and the shreyffes; ys name was
[master Fowler, alias Branch]; he was a monke of Ely: and
ther was a goodly sermon, and after he was cast and con-
demnyd to have ys hand that hurt the prest cut off or he
shuld suffer,[3] and after dysgracyd, and after cared to
Nuwgatt. . . .

The xxiiij day of Aprell was the sam man cared to
Westmynster that dyd hurt the prest, and had ys hand
stryken of at the post, and after he was bornyd aganst sant
Margett chyrche with-owt the cherche-yerde.

From *The Life of Bishop Fisher* [4]

(?) *London.* 1555–8.

. . . the kinge [5] came thither, and was openly sett in his
Chayre to heare the iudgment,[6] where all their proceedings
and actes were openly read in latine: That done, the kinges

---

[1] Clove.   [2] Arraigned.   [3] Before he should suffer death.

[4] Anonymous.   As a human document has a high value, and the
style possesses a clarity and flexibility uncommon in the prose of
the time.

[5] Henry VIII.   [6] Concerning his divorce from Queen Catherine.

Counsell called for iudgment: with that said Cardinal
Campeius [1] in latin, 'No, not so, I will geve no sentence till
I have made relation vnto the Pope of all our doings, whose
commandment I will observe in this Case; the matter is to
high for vs to define hastely, considering the highness of the
persons, and the doubtfull argumentes alleadged, remem-
bringe also whose commissioners we be, and vnder whose
authoritie we sitt, it were (me thinketh) good reason we
should make our cheef head of counsell therwith, before
we proceede to sentence definitive.   I come not hither
to please, for favour, meede [2] or dreed [3] of any person alive,
be he kinge or subiect, neither have I such respect to the
person, that I will offend my conscience or displease god.
I am now an ould man, both weake and sicklye, and daily
looke for death; and should I nowe put my soul in daunger
of gods displeasure to my euerlastinge damnacion for the
favour or feare of any prince in this worlde?   My cominge
hither is only to see iustice ministred accordinge to my
conscience.

From *The Life of Bishop Fisher*

(?) *London*.   1555-8.

    . . . he [Bishop Fisher] setteth his booke immediatly
forth, for a warninge to all posteritie, with a preface before
yt, to his ould acquaintance, the Bishop of Elie, named
Doctor West, being both brought vp together from their
youth in studie at Cambrige . . . the inscription of which
booke was thus: A defence of the kinge of Englands assertion of the Catholick faith against Martin Luthers booke
of the Captiuitie of Babulon.

[1] Cardinal Campeggio.   [2] Meed, reward.   [3] Dread, fear.

. . . Thus lamenting with himself the present state of things, and devising how to provide remedie for that which he sawe followinge, lyke to a carefull Shepherde he laid watch in everie corner, searching all places where the enemye might enter, and where any came within his reach, he tooke houlde on them. . . . Besides, forth he sent abroade certain other preachers, men well instructed to catch the woolfe and to admonish the people of the secrett poyson that laye hidd under pretext of reformacion. But behould, how easie a thinge it is to deceive the sillie [1] people . . . for they, geving care to slaunderous tales and pernitious lyes develishly invented by Luther . . . were fallen in that wilfull blindnes, that making themselves iudges in that which they should receive iudgment of their pastors, nether by the kings assertion against Luther, nether by the continewall visitacions of their byshopps, neither yet by the dilligent and faithfull teaching of the learned fathers and doctors, could be staide, . . . they suffred themselves to be abused by that false and wicked heretick . . . and imbraced him as a trewe and syncere reformer of vice.

From Henry Machyn's *Diary*

London.   *29th April and 1st May* 1559.

The furst day of May ther was ij pennys [2] was dekyd with stremars, baners, and flages, and trumpetes and drumes and gones, gahyng [3] a Mayng, and a-ganst the Quen plasse at Westmynster, and ther they shott and thruw eges [4] and oregns [5] on a-gaynst a-nodur, and with sqwybes, and by chanse on fell on a bage of gune-powdur and sett dyvers men a fyre, and so the men drue to on syd of the penus, and

[1] Simple.   [2] Pinnaces.   [3] Going.
     [4] Eggs.   [5] Oranges.

yt dyd over-swelmed the pennus, and mony fell in the Temes, butt, thanke be God, ther was but on man drownyd, and a C. bottes [1] abowtt here, and the Quen grace and her lordes and lades lokyng out of wyndows; thys was done by ix of the cloke on May evyn last.

The xxix day of Aprell [2] at Dowgatt in London ther was a mayd dwelling with master Cotyngham, on of the quen pulters [3]; the mayd putt in-to a pott of [4] . . . serten powyssun [5] and browth them unto her mastores, and to iiij of her servandes, and they dyd ett them; and as sone as they had ett them thay be-gane to swell and to vomett peteusle [6]; and ther cam a good woman causyd to be feychyd serten dolle [7] of salett owylle to drynke, and thanke be to God they be-gayne to mend and never one ded of ytt. . . . . thes ij persunes have dullysly [8] gyffen poyssun [to their] mastores and ther howshold, and ether of them ij handes cute off.

From Henry Machyn's *Diary*

London.   *Feb.* 1562/3—*June* 1563.

The xxij day of Feybruary was Shroyff-monday, at Charyng-crosse ther was a man cared of iiij men, and a-for hym a bagpype playing, a shame [9] and a drum playhyng, and xx lynkes [10] bornyng a-bowtt hym, because ys next neybor wyff ded bett [11] here hosband; ther-for yt [is] ordered that ys next naybor shall ryd a-bowtt the plase. . . .

The iiij day [of] Marche ther was a mans dowther dwellyng

---

[1] Boats.   [2] This is the order in the MS.
[3] Poulterers.   [4] So MS.   [5] Poison.
[6] Piteously.   [7] Portion, amount.   [8] Devilishly.
[9] Shawm.   [10] Torches.   [11] Beat.

in sant James in Garlyke heyff,[1] in the plase that w[as the] yerle of Wosetur plase, she was delevered with a chyld, and after caste yt owt of a wyndow in-to Temes. . . .

The vii day of Aprell at sant Katheryns be-yond the Towre the wyff of the syne of the Rose, a tavarne, was set on the pelere for ettyng of rowe [2] flesse and rostyd boyth,[3] and iiij women was sett in the stokes all nyght tyll ther hosbandes dyd feyche them hom. . . . The xvj day of June dyd ryd in a care [to the] yeld-hall docthur Langton the phesyssyon in a g[own] of damaske lynyd with velvett and a cott of velvett . . . and a cape of velvett, and he had pynd a bluw ho[od on] cape,[4] and so cam thrugh Chepe-syd on the market [day,] and so a-bowtt London, for [he] was taken with ij wenchys yonge a-tones.[5] . . . The xix day of June yt raynyd swett showrs tyll x of the cloke.

From a Petition presented by Parliament to Queen Elizabeth, urging her to debar Mary Queen of Scots from succession to the English Crown

London.   *May* 1572

. . . That . . . Mary, daughter and heire of Jeames the fifte, late Kinge of Scottes, commonly called Queene of Scottes, most wickedly, falsely, and unjustly hath claymed the present state and possession of your royall crowne of your realme of England and Ireland . . . and the same her said false and pretended title shee hath by her ministeres and faintours [6] from tyme to tyme practised sondrye wayes to preferre, sett forward, advaunce, and publishe . . . ;

---

[1] Garlickhithe.   [2] Raw (i.e. during Lent).   [3] Both, i.e. also.

[4] The mark of disgrace, for adultery; cape=cap.

[5] Together.

[6] An unexampled form. Perhaps a hybrid from (i) *fainours*, pretenders. See OED *Feign. II.* 5, and (ii) confusion with *fautors*, adherents; hence, those who supported her pretended title; or else an error for *fawtors, fautors*.

H

And for better setting forward of all the fond trayterous intencions . . . certaine rebells and traytours to your Majestie . . . have both in bookes and petigrees [1] deduced unto the said Mary a false, pretenced [2] and colorable tytle by discent to your Majesties crowne . . . ;

And allthoughe your Majestie of your most aboundaunt goodnes hath hitherto, above the common limittes and bondes of mercye forborne to procead against the said Mary accordinge to her deservinge . . . yet nowe, seing her malice to be nothing restrayned with due consideration of your Majesties goodnes . . . towardes her, at whose handes shee hath receaved great and sondry benefittes and namely [3] . . . the salfegarde [4] and preservacion of her lyfe, which should have bene taken from her in the realme of Scottland for sondry horrible crymes wherwith shee was then chardged, if your Highnes most kinde . . . mediacion . . . on her behalfe had not wrought her salftye;

And considering also the most wicked and malicious devices . . . of her and her confederates and fantours [5] towardes your Majestie do not cease but dayly encrease . . . wee therefore, your true and obedient subjectes . . . do most humbly beseeche your Majestie . . . not to beare in vayne the swerde of justice. . . .

The Bardon Papers.

From Gosson's *Schoole of Abuse*
London.   1579.

How often hath her Maiestie . . . sette downe the limits of apparell to euery degree, and how soone againe hath the pride of our harts ouerflowen the chanel? . . . Ouerlashing [6]

[1] Pedigrees, genealogical tables.   [2] Pretended.
[3] Especially.   [4] Safeguard.   [5] See n. 6, p. 93.   [6] Extravagance.

in apparel is so common a fault that the very hyerlings of some of our Players, which stand at reuersion of vi s. by the weeke, iet [1] vnder Gentlemens noses in sutes of silke, exercising themselues too [2] prating on the stage, and common scoffing when they come abrode.[3] . . . I speake not this, as though euerye one that professeth the qualitie so abused him selfe, for it is well knowen that some of them are . . . properly learned honest housholders and Citizens . . . though the pryde of their shadowes (I meane those hangebyes [4] whom they succour with stipend) cause them to bee somewhat il talked of abroade. And as some of the Players are farre from abuse: so some of their Playes are without rebuke. . . . These Playes are good playes and sweete playes . . . woorthy to bee soung of the Muses. . . .

Now if any man aske me why my selfe haue penned Comedyes in time paste, and inueigh so egerly against them here, let him knowe that *Semel insaniuimus omnes*: I have sinned, and am sorry for my fault. . . . I gaue my self to that exercise in hope to thriue, but I . . . lost bothe my time and my trauell [5] when I had doone.

Thus sith I haue in my voyage suffred wrack [6] with Vlisses, and wringing-wet scrambled with life to the shore, stand from mee Nausicaä with all thy traine, till I wipe the blot from my forhead, and with sweet springs wash away the salt froath [7] that cleaues too my soule.

From Gosson's *Schoole of Abuse*
London. 1579.

From the head to the foote, from the top to the toe, there should nothing be vaine, no body idle. Iupiter himself

---

[1] Swagger. [2] To. [3] Abroad, out-of-doors. [4] 'Hangers-on.'
[5] Travail, effort. [6] Wreck. [7] Forth.

shall stand for example, who is euer in woork, still moouing and turning about the heauens, if he shuld pull his hand from the frame, it were impossible for the world to indure. All would be day, or al night; All spring or all Autume; . . . no time to plant, no time to reape, the earth barren, the riuers stopt, the Seas stayde, the seasons chaunged, and the whole course of nature ouerthrowen. . . .

If it be the dutie of euery man in a common wealth, one way or other to bestirre his stumpes, I cannot but blame those lither [1] contemplators very much, which sit concluding of Sillogismes in a corner, which in a close study in the Vniuersity coope themselues vp fortie yeres togither studying all thinges, and professe nothing. The Bell is knowen by his sounde, the Byrde by her voyce, the Lyon by his rore, the Tree by the fruits, a man by his woorkes. . . . No man is borne to seeke priuate profite.

From Dr. Dee's *Diary*

Mortlake (Surrey)   1581–8.

1581. March 8th it was the 8 day being Wensday, hora noctis 10–11, the strange noyse in my chamber of knocking; and the voyce, ten tymes repeted, somewhat like the shrich of an owle, but more longly drawn and more softly, as it were in my chamber.

1583. Jan. 13th, on Sonday the stage at Paris Garden fell down all at ones, being full of people beholding the bear-bayting. Many being killed thereby, more hart, and all amased. The godly expownd it as a due plage of God for the wickednes ther usid, and the Sabath day so profanely spent. . . .

---

[1] Lazy, easy-going. OE. *lýðer* ;

Jan. 23rd, the Ryght Honorable Mr. Secretary Walsing-
ham cam to my howse, where by good lok he found Mr.
Awdrian Gilbert, and so talk was begonne of North-west
Straights discovery. . . .

1588. Jan. 1st, abowt nine of the clok afternone, Michel,[1]
going chilyshly with a sharp stik of eight ynches long and a
little wax candell light on the top of it, did fall uppon the
playn bords in Maries chamber, and the sharp point of the
stik entred throwgh the lid of his left ey toward the corner
next the nose, and so persed throwgh, insomuch that great
abundance of blud cam out under the lid, in the very corner
of the sayd eye; the hole on the owtside is not bygger then
a pyns hed; it was anoynted with St. Johns oyle. The boy
slept well. God spede the rest of the cure!

From QUEEN ELIZABETH,

To KING JAMES VI OF SCOTLAND

London. *March* 1585/6.

The expertist seamen, my deare brother, makes vant of
ther best shippes whan the [2] pas the highest bellowes
without yelding, and broke nimlest [3] the roughest stormes.
The like profe, I suppose, may best be made, and surest
boste, of frindes, whan greatest persuasions and mightiest
ennemis oppose themselues for parties. If than a constant
irremouable good wyll appere, thar is best triall made.
And for that I knowe ther is no worse orator for truthe than
malice, nor shwredar invahar [4] than envye, and that I am
sure you have wanted nether to assaile your mynde to win
it from our frindeship, if not auailing all thes minars,[5]
you kipe the hold of your promised inward affection, as

[1] One of his small sons.   [2] They.   [3] Most swiftly, 'nimblest.'
[4] Shrewder inveigher.   [5] Lighthouses, <*Sp. minarete.*

Randol [1] at lengthe haue told me, and your owne lettars assure me, I dare thus boldly affirme that you shall haue the bettar part in this bargain. For when you way in equal balance, with no palsey hand, the very ground of ther desires that wold withdrawe you, it is but roote of mischif to peril your selfe, with hope to harme her who euer hathe preserued you; and sins you may be sure that Skotland, nor yourself, be so potent, as for your greatnes the [2] seake you, nor neuer did, but to iniure a thirde; and if you rede the histories, ther is no great cause of bost for many conquests, thogh your contry sarued ther malice. This you see the beginning why euer Skotland hath bine sought. Now, to come to my ground worke, only natural affection *ab incunabulis* sturrid me to saue you from the murderars of your father and the peril that ther complices [3] might brede you.[4] . . . And as I reioyse to haue had, iven in this hammering worlde, suche present profe of your sincerite, so shal you be sure to imploye it upon no gileful person, nor suche as wil not take as muche regard of your good as of her owne. . . .

Your most assured louinge sistar and cousin,

Elizabeth R.

The Letters of Queen Elizabeth and James VI.

From Lord Burghley [5]

To Sir Christopher Hatton [6]

London.   *4th Sept.* 1586.

Sir, I hartely thank yow for your comfortable lettre so effectvally expressyng hir Majesties kyndnes in allowyng of

---

[1] Randolph.   [2] They.   [3] Their accomplices.   [4] Breed for you.

[5] Secretary of State, and afterwards Treasurer.

[6] Vice-chamberlain, Captain of the Guard, and Privy Counsellor to Queen Elizabeth.

my servyce, being not answerable to my dvty but in good will, and in favoryng me from labor with my evill foote, which notwithstandyng is and shall be with the rest of my body withovt any respect of payn, at all commandmentes for her service.   I will expect your commyng at my Lord Chancellors at 2 on Mondaye.   Sence your departvr Dvn,[1] that lay so long in the myre withovt styrryng, keppyng silence obstinatly, hath withovt any torment offred, liberally confessed as much as we conceaved hym gilty of. He maketh larg [2] reportes of all the practises, shvnning in phrases as much as he can to accuse hym self of his own maliciovss purpooss, othar than of his knowledg of the whole and that largly.   The 2 Abyngtons [3] ar taken in a shepehoues in Herefordshyr neare Seaborns houss.

I thynk Naw and Curle [4] will yeld in ther wrytyng soomwhat to confirm ther Mastriss crymes, but if they war perswaded that them selves might scape, and the blow fall uppon ther Mistriss, betwixt hir head and hir shulders, suerly we shold have the whole from [hem].

If yow shall bryng any more wrytyng with yow from thence to towch both Naw, Curle and Pasquyre,[5] it shall serve vs the better, and spare our threatninges to them. . . .

[1] Henry Donn, one of the conspirators in Babington's plot.

[2] Complete.

[3] Edward and Thomas Habington, both conspirators in Babington's Plot, and sons of John Habington, cofferer to Queen Elizabeth. They were said to have been caught in a hay-mow near their father's house in Worcestershire, and not in a sheepfold as Burghley states here.

[4] Claude Nau and Gilbert Curle, secretaries of Mary Queen of Scots.

[5] One of Mary's servants.

From my houss at Westminster, wrytt in my bed, but with intent to ryse and to be occupied.   4 Sept., 1586.

Yours so bovnd,

W. BURGHLEY.

The Bardon Papers.

From QUEEN ELIZABETH

To KING JAMES VI OF SCOTLAND

London.   *May* 1588.

[1] My pen, my deare brother, hathe remained so long dry as I suppose hit hardly wold have taken ynke again, but, mollefied by the good justice that with your owne person you have bine pleased to execute, togither with the large assurance that your wordes have given to some of my ministars, wiche all dothe make me ready to drinke most willingly a large draught of the rivar of Lethe, never minding to thinke of unkindnes, but to turne my yees [2] to the making vp of that sure amitie and stanche good wyll wiche may be presently concluded in ending our league. . . .

I have millions of thankes to rendar you, that so frankely told to Cary suche offers as wer made to you,[3] wiche I doute not but you shall euer haue cause to reioyse that you refuse; for wher the [4] meane to weken your surest frind, so be you assured the intended to subiect you and yours. For you see how the deale euen with ther owne in al countries lessar than ther one,[5] and therfor God, for your best, I assure myselfe wil not let you faule into suche an aperte daunger, undar the cloke, for al that, of harming

[1] Written after some time of estrangement between Elizabeth and James, after the death of Mary Queen of Scots.

[2] Eyes.   [3] i.e. offers of alliance made by Spain.

[4] They.   [5] Own.

other [1] and aduansing you; but I hope you wil take Ulisses wexe [2] to saue you from suche sirenes. . . .

If I deserue not your amitie, persecute me as your foe; but being yours, use me like a prince who feareth none but God.

Your most assured loving sistar and cousin,

ELIZABETH R.

The Letters of Queen Elizabeth and James VI.

From QUEEN ELIZABETH,

To KING JAMES VI OF SCOTLAND

London. *Jan.* 1591/2.

My deare brother, Thogh the heringe of your most daungerous peril [3] be that thing that I most reuerently rendar my most lowly thankes to God that you, by his mighty hand, hath skaped, yet hathe hit bine no other hazard than suche as bothe hathe bine forsien and fortold; but Cassandra was neuer credited til the mishap had rather chanched [4] than was prevented. The poore man who, against his wyl, was intercepted with all suche epistelz as traitors sent and receved, was for reward put to the bootes [5]; so litel was any thing regarded that procided from your best friend, and yet the matter made to [6] aparant, or [7] many days after, throw [8] the traiterous assembly of your euidant rebelz, that with banner displaied and again [9] you in the fild. Thes wer the calendes of this late attempt. I knowe not what to write, so litel do I like to loose labor in vaine;

---

[1] Others. [2] Wax.

[3] James was attacked in Holyrood by Bothwell and his followers.

[4] 'Chanced,' come to pass. [5] A form of torture. [6] Too.

[7] Ere. [8] Through. [9] Against.

for if I saw counsel auaill, or aught pursued in due time or season, I shuld thinke my time fortunatly spent to make you reape the due fruit of right oportunitie; but I see you haue no luk [1] to helpe your state, nor to assure you from tresons leasur.[2] You giue to muche respit to rid your harme and shorten others hast.[3] Wel, I wyl pray for you, that God wyl unseal your yees, that to [4] long haue bin shut, and do require you thinke that none shal more joy therat than myselfe, that most I am sure grives [5] the contrary. . . . Praying God to defend you from all mishap or treason,

Your most assured loving sistar and cousin,

ELIZABETH R.

The Letters of Queen Elizabeth and James VI.

From QUEEN ELIZABETH,

TO KING JAMES VI OF SCOTLAND

London.   *May* 1593.

. . . And, now, I heare that some nobleman [6] hath bine accused of so horrible a crime as my hart rues to remember. For Godz loue, look throw no spectacles to your owne safety. Your yees be younge, you nideth not haue a clere sight in your so nye a cause, and let your counseil see that you wyl not easely be begiled in making to smal regard of that wiche toucheth life—yea, of a king! For overgreat audacitie wyl brede,[7] to a mynde that may be sone perswaded that all is wel, to do the boldlar [8] a wicked act.

---

[1] Desire, 'like.'   [2] ? harm, injury; see OED. s.v. *Lesure.*
[3] Haste.   [4] Too.   [5] Grieves.
[6] Probably a reference to an attempt made on James's life by Clunie Crichtoun (see Calderwood, *History of the Kirk of Scotland*).
[7] Breed.   [8] More boldly.

Hard is the skul [1] that may serue in place of suche a danger, nay, hit may bride [2] hit to neglect hit. You haue had many treasons wiche to tendarly you haue wrapt vp. I pray God the cindars of suche a fire bride not one day your ruine. God is witnes I malice none, but for your seurty is only the care of my writing. I desiar no bloude, but God saue yours. Only this my long experience teacheth me; whan a king neglectes himself, who wyl make them [3] enemis for him? Let this serve you for a *caveat*. You wil beare with the fault that affection commiteth, and use the profit to your best good. For wiche I wyl euer pray to God, who long defend you from al treachery.

Your most assured loving sistar and cousin,

ELIZABETH R.

The Letters of Queen Elizabeth and James VI.

From Dr. Dee's *Diary*

Mortlake (Surrey).   *Feb.* 1593/4 *to June* 1594.

1593. Feb. 22nd, a sharp anger betwene me and the Bishop of Leightyn in the towr, for that he wold not shew his farder interest to Nangle; he sayd that after I had seen his brode seal of commendation, that I had institution and induction to the Nangle. Then I sayd his lordship did fable. He there uppon that so moved that he called me spitefully 'coniver.' I told him that he did lye in so saying, and that I wold try on the fleysh of him, or by a bastaned [4] gown of him, if he wer not prisoner in the Tower. Inter 12ª et 2ª a meridie my sharp anger with the Bishop of

---

[1] ? skill, ability; see OED. sv. *Skill*, sb.¹   [2] Breed.   [3] Themselves.

[4] An unexampled form. Perhaps (i) < *baste*, to sew loosely; see OED. *Baste. Flesh-baste*, [*Flesh. III*, 13]. (ii) for *bastoned*, < *baston*, a cudgel. (iii) an erroneous form of *bastard*, a coarse cloth, or gown of unusual make or size. I have been unable to find any proverbial saying of this kind recorded.

Leightyn in the lieftenantes dyning parlor before the
Lieutenant Sir Michael Blunt. Mr. Liewtenat Nant and
Mr. Blunt are wittnesses. . . .

May 21st, be it remembered that on this xxj day of May
I bargayned with and bowght of Mr. Mark Perpoint, of
Mortlak, that next mansion howse with the plat and all
the appertenances abowt it for £32. . . .

1594. June 29th, after I had hard the Archbishop his
answers and discourses and that after he had byn the last
Sonday at Tybalds [1] with the Quene and Lord Threasorer, I
take myself confounded for all suing or hoping for anything
that was. And so adiew to the court and courting tyll
God direct me otherwise! The Archbishop gave me a payre
of sufferings [2] to drinke. God be my help as he is my
refuge! Amen.

From QUEEN ELIZABETH,
    To KING JAMES VI OF SCOTLAND [3]

London.   *4th Jan.* 1597/8.

When the first blast of a strange vnvsed and sild [4] hard
of sounde had pearsed my ears, I supposed that flyeing
fame, who with swift quills ofte paseth with the worst, had
brought report of some untrothe. . . .

I doe wonder what evyll spiritts have possest you, to set
forthe so infamous devyses void of any shewe of trothe.
I am sorry that you have so wilfully falen from your best
stay, and will needs throwe yourself into the hurlpole [5] of
bottomles discreditt. Was the hast soe great to hye to

---

[1] Theobalds, Burghley's seat at Cheshunt, Herts.

[2] A couple of sovereigns.

[3] This letter refers to some words spoken by James in his Parliament about Elizabeth.

[4] Seldom.   [5] Whirlpool.

such oprobry, as that you would pronounce a never-thought-of action afore you had but asked the question of her that best could tell it?   I see well wee two be of very different natures, for I vowe to God I would not corrupt my tonge with an vnknowen report of the greatest foe I have, muche lesse could I detract my best-deserving freinde with a spott so fowle as scarsly may ever be out-raised. . . .

Though not right, yet salve some peece of this overslypp. And be assured, that you deale with such a kinge as will beare no wronges and indure infamy.   The examples have ben so lately seen, as they can hardly be forgotten, of a farr mightier and potenter prince than many Europe hathe.[1] Looke you not therefore that without large amends I may or will slupper-up [2] such indignities. . . . And so I re-comend you to a better mynde and more advysed con-clusions. . . .

Your more redyer sister than your self hathe done, for that is fitt,

ELIZABETH R.

The Letters of Queen Elizabeth and James VI.

From NICHOLAS SQUYER,

To JOHN WILLOUGHBY

Cornwall and London.   *22nd Nov.* 1600.

Mr. Willowby.   I wrote to you consarning Ser Gorges Cary [3] his comming for Eingland the same time I wrote to my brother.   I have now receved a letter from my brother, but no answer of the letter thatt I sentt him that tim,

---

[1] A reference to the defeat of the Armada.
[2] Gloss over; see OED. s.v. *Slubber*, vb. 4.   [3] Sir George Cary.

tharfor I doute that the [1] never cam to youer hands. Ser
Gorges had leve to com for Eingland the firste of this
monthe, but he was commanded agane to staye befor my
Lord Debette [2] cam home to Deblyn,[3] for he hath ben in
the northe a grete whill, and hath don grete sarves [4] thar;
so by this time I thinke he is come home, for Ser Gorges
hath sente over all his horsses, but only [5] his fotcloth nige,[6]
and as moche of his stoufe as doth lode a carte, and is
landed at Chester, so I hope it well nott be longe before
he be hear [7] himselfe, and doth mean to se Devonsher as
sone as he can, and meanes not to go over no more if he can
be descharged.   No more at this tim, but my very harty
commendacion to youer selfe and to youer wife.   I end,
from Mr. Carmorden's house in Marke lane in London, the
xxijth of November.

Youer to his pouer,

NICHOLAS SQUYER.

The Trevelyan Papers.

From LADY ANN TOWNSHEND,

To MR. MASON of London

Stiffkey (Norfolk).   *27th Dec.* 1601.

Sr, although I can not shewe my thankfulnes as I would
to my Lady Bartlet for hir late great favor, yet I hope of hir
honerabell acceptans of my willinge minde, and as a token
of the same I am boulde to present her ho.[8] wth 2 Tur-
kyes, and a Phesant, 7 brace of Patriges and halfe a dosen
greene plover w[ch] I have sent by this bearar, Brooke, w[ch]

---

[1] They.   [2] Lord Deputy (of Ireland), (Lord Mountjoy).

[3] Dublin.   [4] Service.   [5] Except.

[6] ? Sumpter-horse (? nag); I have been unable to trace any form
of *nig*, meaning nag; cf. *neg*; see OED. s.v. *Nag*.

[7] Here.   [8] Honour.

I humble [1] pray hir ho. to accepte, wth a fewe puddinges
and linkes [2] for a breackfast to my brother Sr. Roberd,
yourselfe, and my sunn Roger.   I wish them worthy your
eatinge.   Time will not suffer me to writ to my Lady as I
would, for wch cause I am bould to trobell you.   My
children are both well, I thank God, but my selfe much
trobled wth an extreame coulde.   It is so late as [3] I am
forsed to eande.[4]   The Pheasant and Patridg are very
newe, and Plovers as I was towld: my puddinges are not so
good I think as they have bene, wch I am sory for, but now
can not healpe.   So commending me very kindly unto you,
praying you to remember my humbell duty to my La.[5]
wth many and great thankes unto hir ho. for all hir kind-
neses to me and mine.   My daughter and sunn hath both
of them sent a leatter to my Lady.   Puss hath made 2
latten verses wth hir other exercises in one daye; she
mackes an eand of learning at ouer Lady.[6]   I am forsed
to eand unwillingly, resting ever

Your most assured frinde,

ANN TOWNSHENDE.

The Stiffkey Papers.

From NICHOLAS SQUYER,

To JOHN WILLOUGHBY

Cornwall and London.   *17th May* 1602.

Good Mr. Willowby.   I ded write to you neare aboute
Easter the answer of youer kinde letter you wrote unto me.
For the whiche I geve you moste harty thankes, which I
hoope will com to som good perficcion,[7] when Ser George

---

[1] Humbly.   [2] Sausages.   [3] Here=that.
[4] End.   [5] Lady.   [6] i.e. she finishes schooling on Lady Day.
[7] Perfection.

doth com into England, which will be aboute Michellmas, and not befoor. Butt then he will staye heare all the wenter,[1] and we hoope that he will nott go over any moor.

Thar is no nuse out of Ierland but good. My Lord Debety is now goinge up to the Tarons [2] contary, and there is more solders goeth over forthewithe; heare hath ben suche a prese [3] in London for the Lowe Contery [4] that the licke was never sene in Eingland: the ded [5] prese earles, barrons, knightes, justesses of the peese and gentelmen, and all other sortes of men . . . and contery men that had suttes in lawe.[6]   All these sortes of pepell taken up in the stretes . . . and so sente to the shepes; the could not be suffred to goo to thar owen howses or lodgins: but whear thar wàs a thousant preste, thar was nott aboufe thre hondered ded sarve, but weare sente bake agane, for thar was complents mad to the consell, and so thar was ordar takinge [7] that the should prese non but suche as dwelte within the cety and cebarbes [8]: and these that wear masterles men, conny catchers [9] and suche licke, and that was the true meaning of the firste prese.   My mistress would knowe what mones [10] is dewe to her in youer hand, and what hath ben bestowed thar sethens [11] we came from thens.

I end, commetten [12] you to Good.[13]   From Holborn, the xvijth of Maye.

Youer to his poor power,

NICHOLES SQUYER.

The Trevelyan Papers.

---

[1] Winter.   [2] Tyrone's.   [3] Press (military conscription).
[4] i.e. for soldiers to serve in Holland.   [5] They did.
[6] Suits at law.   [7] Taken (pp.).   [8] Suburbs.
[9] Cheats, sharpers, welshers, etc.   [10] moneys.
[11] Since (OE. *siððanes*).   [12] Committing.   [13] God.

From HUMPHRY SPURWAY,

To JOHN WILLOUGHBY

Cornwall and London.   *28th Jan.* 1605.

Good Mr. Willoughbie.   Sir George Carye is nott come oute of Irelande, but there is a messinger gone unto him sithence Mrs. Allingtons deathe, and it is thoughte that he wilbe here shortelie.   I ame promised to hier as soon as there ys anie retorne from him, and then shall you hier more from me.   Itt is thoughte there wilbe a Parliamente aboute Marche, yf God staye the sicknes,[1] whereof there is greate hope, for there dyed butt xiiij^tenn this weeke in the plauge.[1]   There hath beene a disputation before the kinge, who was moderator, betwene the Buishopes and the Mynisters, wherupon there are manie controversies betwene them agreed one,[2] and it is thoughte that there shalbe a learned mynistery established, and ytt is fully agreed againste pluralityes.   Newse here is litle, onely West-minstre hale [3] ys very gaunte.[4]   And soe, wishinge you and good Mrs. Willoughbie all good fortune, I comite you to God.   Inner Temple, the xxviijth of Januarye, 1605.

Yours alwaies assured,

HUMFRY SPURWAYE.

The Trevelyan Papers.

From GEORGE TREVELYAN,

To his father, JOHN TREVELYAN

Cornwall and London.   19*th July* 1606.

Right worthy Father,—My duty in all reverense I kyndly presente, hoping you will accepte those laynes [5] from your

---

[1] The plague.   [2] On.

[3] Westminster Hall, where all legal business was transacted.

[4] Empty.   [5] These lines.

I

dutifull soone, who will with his beest indevors labor to continue your fatherly affecttion towardes hym.   And seeing the trobelles of my Lo: pretended jurny [1] willes me not to be teadiose, I beseech you to pardon me for my brevitie in writing at this presente, and upon our retorne I will not fayll to sertify you of all busines what soever; in the meane tyme I pray you to be a pertaker of oure happy nuse, which is that ore [2] Lady Chicester is conseved withe childe, the which God grant it to be a soone, that he may ineryte, and be a joye to his parentes in there elder eyres.[3]

Sir, in my last letters I gave you to understand that his ho^r Lo: [4] intended to procure the warde of Massarene, and to bestow it upon me, which determynation he continues, and at the retorne from ore jurny his Lo: will assure it by patton [5] if porsabell [6] he may. . . .

Sir, you may imagen that I played the yell [7] hosband with the monyes I had of you, but to free my seelfe from all suspitions, I assure you that, at my comming from Nectellcombe,[8] I had but one xxx[8] left of all the mony you gave me: for the rest I payd it to a frynd which I had borood of before. . . . So beseeching you for this tyme to satesfy my request in hombell manner, and with my loweall [9] duty to my mother and your seelfe, in all hast I am forst to end, but ever to remayne,

> Your true obedient sonne to the
>> owre of death,
>>> GEORGE TREVYLIAN.
>>> *The Trevelyan Papers.*

---

[1] My lord's intended journey.   [2] Our.   [3] Years.
[4] Honour(able) lordship.   [5] Patent.   [6] Possible.
[7] Ill.   [8] Nettlecombe.   [9] Loyal.

From George Trevelyan,

To his father, John Trevelyan

Cornwall and London.   *11th Feb.* 1612.

My honorabell Father,—This barer, owre cosen Trevelian, having more occation to use mony in England than
here, hath left me a commodity of cloth which I coold
hardly geett for my use in these partes, which amountes
to the some of fyve poundes forteene shillinges, the which
I must intreate you to disborce [1] for my use upon the
reseate of this my letter. . . .

Honorabell Sir, although our nobell Knight Martiall [2] is
retorned out of England, yett can I nott give you full
satesfaction in every poyntt though the hoole busynes be
lefte to the disposing of owre honorabell good Lo.   I meane
the busynes of the Murrowes,[3] which I sentt you . . . in
my last letters . . . by my cosen Frances Bassett, whose
brother and my seelfe, with som others besydes, are chowsen
commitioners by my Lords appoyntment to take a nue
survaye of those landes, and to se all mens proportiones
strickly [4] mesured according to the shayres [5] they ar like
to inioy.   Wee have halfe a promyce from his Lordp. for
one thousand acers a peese, but one [6] what conditions I am
nott abell to resoullfe [7] you. . . .

So, craving pardon for my falltes, and for nott writing
to any of my frindes besydes, in all hast . . .

Your dutefull and obedient sone,

George Trevelian.

The Trevelyan Papers.

[1] Disburse.

[2] Knight Marshal (of Ireland) Sir Richard Wingfield.

[3] The Murrowes, a district in Co. Wexford, granted by Privy
Seals to George Trevelyan.

[4] Strictly.   [5] Shares.   [6] On.   [7] Resolve.

From *Newes from London*, 1618

London.   *2nd Nov.* 1618.

S^r. W. Rawleigh was executed in the old Pallace at Westminster, Thursday last,[1] whose manner of dying won him more love then I can express.

The cause of his sudden dying is expected to be published by some book warranted by our State.

The French agent is dismissed and sent home. Some likelihood there is of a breach between us and them.

The divines sent into the Lowe Cuntreyes are not yet returned, but expected this next week.

The Lady Rawleighe on Wednesday night last made suit to the Co^rs [2] to sup with her husband that night, and to have the dead body of her husband the next day, both which were willingly granted her.

The Sweathen [3] Kinge hath overthrown the Poland, and killed their King [4] in the feild. . . .

The accomptants to the King are all eagerly call'd upon, and what they owe must be presently [5] paid, which makes many a good man to pinch, to their great hurt and damage.

The Turkishe Embassador, or rather a messenger, hath his audience tomorrow.

                                   The Trevelyan Papers.

From DOROTHY BACON,

          To her grandson, SIR NATHANIEL BACON

Stiffkey (*Norfolk*).   *21st June, c.* 1622.

Sir, I have had full spech with my sistar Hubart conserneng the menestar wch leves in hir house, and shee saith

---

[1] 29th October.   [2] Commissioners (of the Tower).
[3] Sweden (i.e. Swedish), Gustavus Adolphus.
[4] Sigismund III.   [5] Immediately.

that hee is a very well condecoyned [1] mane, fry [2] from all wiesses,[3] wch y^t [4] house a fordeth, and so mild a ·humbell harted mane as can be, and my sistar hath heard him prech at Plumsted to his much commendacyons, more, that shee hath heard the Prechar ther and othars besides report of him to be a very good scollar. He is a master of Artt and did Red [5] to her Eilldest [6] sonne, but now beyng gonne shee thinkes him to be at libarty: so as yf y^u plese to except of this mane my sistar doth beleve y^u shall nevr have case to Repent y^u. My sistar did much commend Mr. Day to me before I heard from you, and wised [7] him a place out of that house, for hee is worthy to be wher he maye be Respeckted and Ewsed [8] as a mecke [9] mane, for shee sayth that yf Inquyry be made a bout Plumsted of him, it wold be sonne senne [10] how well beloved hee is, and how glad many ther wold be to hear of his Preferment. I had wrytten this letar I hear [11] send to y^u that y^u maye send yf y^u plese aftar you have Red it, but my sistar doutted that the Prechar dar not deall in it for fear of Sir Thomas Hubart, yt [12] me thinkes yf the mane be at his lebarty what ned hee care for his good will, and this,[13] Sire, I wish y^u had anye greatar matar wherin I might dooe you anye good, and with my sistars and my dew Respects to y^r selfe, I so Rest as

Your very loveng granmothar,

DOROTHE BACON.

The Stiffkey Papers.

[1] Well-conditioned. [2] Free. [3] Vices. [4] That.
[5] Read, i.e. tutor. [6] Eldest. [7] Wished.
[8] Used, treated. [9] Meek, godly. [10] Soon seen.
[11] Here. [12] Yet. [13] Thus.

From LADY BRILLIANA HARLEY,

To her husband, SIR ROBERT HARLEY

Bucks and Herefordshire.   *5th Oct,* 1627.

Deare Sʳ.—Your two leters, on from Hearifort [1] and the other from Gloster, weare uery wellcome to me: and if you knwe howe gladly I reseaue your leters, I beleeue you would neeuer let any opertunity pase.   I hope your cloche [2] did you saruis betwne Gloster and my brother Brays, for with vs it was a very rainy day, but this day has bine very dry and warme, and so I hope it was with you; and to morowe I hope you will be well at your journis end, wheare I wisch my self to bide you wellcome home.   You see howe my thoughts goo with you: and as you haue many of mine, so let me haue some of yours.   Beleeue me, I thinke I neuer miste you more then nowe I doo, or ells I haue forgoot what is past.   I thanke God, Ned and Robin [3] are well; and Ned askes every day wheare you are, and he says you will come to morowe.   My father [4] is well, but goos not abrode, becaus of his fiseke.   I haue sent you vp a litell hamper, in which is the box with the ryteings and boouckes you bide me send vp, with the other things, sowed up in a clothe, in the botome of the hamper.   I haue sent you a partriche pye, which has the two pea chikeins in it, and a litell runlet of meathe, that which I toold you I made for my father. I thinke within this muthe, it will be very good drinke. I sende it vp nowe becaus I thinke carage when it is ready to drincke dous it hurt; thearefore, and please you to let it rest and then taste it; if it be good, I pray you let my father have it, because he spake to me for such meathe.   I will nowe bide you god night, for it is past a leauen a cloke.   I pray God presarue you and giue you

---

[1] Hereford.   [2] Cloak.   [3] Her sons.   [4] Father-in-law.

good sugsess in all your biusnes, and a speady and happy meeting.

> Your most faithfull affectinat wife,
>
> BRILLIANA HARLEY.

I must beeg your bllsing [1] for Ned and Rob, and present you with Neds humbell duty.

> *The Letters of Lady Brilliana Harley.*

From MRS. WISEMAN,

> To LADY VERNEY

Bucks and London.   *20th June* 1629.

Good Madam, I am glad to hear of my neeses [2] marigh with your sonne.[3] I pray God send them as much joye and happines as euer anye cuppell had! I could haue wissed [4] that Sir Edmund Verney would haue settelled his land vpon them, accoring to his promise befor they had bine maried. I make no douth [5] but he will dou it accoringe to his word, otherwise hir frinds will blame Mr. Wiseman and me, whoe weare the case [6] of the mache,[7] and my neece will do the like when shee shall com to vnderstand whatt shee hath done; wherfor, good madam, will you be a means to haue it don, and I will be allways redy to do them any sarues.

I humbelly thanke you for your kind inuitacione: I will haue a tim to wayt on you. Our accasion [8] of bilding this sommer is great, wich will be the let.[9] Good madam, let

---

[1] Blessing.

[2] Mary Blacknall, daughter of John Blacknall of Abingdon. She was fourteen at the time this letter was written.

[3] Ralph Verney.   [4] Wished.   [5] Doubt.   [6] Cause.

[7] Match.   [8] 'Occasion' here=need.   [9] Hindrance, obstacle.

me intreat you that your sonne and daftere [1] may com to Abington, to be better acquinted with ther owne.[2] I desir my seruis and Mr. Wiseman's may be presented to Sir Edmund Verney and your selfe, and our due respecks to all yours. I rest

Your faithfull searuant to searue you,

MARY WISEMAN.

The Verney Memoirs.

From LADY BRILLIANA HARLEY,

To her son, EDWARD

Bucks and Herefordshire.   22nd March 1638.

    . . . My deare Ned, I thanke you for your letter by the carrier this wake. Howe soeuer trubells may befall me, yet if it be well with you, I reioyce. I thanke God, that you injoy your health. The Lord in mercy continue it to you. My deare Ned, I longe to see you; but I feare it will not be a great whille. I know not well when the Acte [3] is, and I thinke I must not looke to see you tell the Act be past. Whensoeuer it is, I beceach the Lord, giue vs a happy seeing on of another. I am sorry my lady Corbet takes no more care of her chilederen. Sr And[re]we Corbet left two thousand pounds a year. Shee has a way that I should not take, by my good will with my chillderen, without it weare to correct some great fallt in them; but my deare Ned, as longe as it pleases God I haue it, I shall willingly giue what is in my power for the beest adwantage of you, and your brothers and sisters, as ocation offers itself. Vse your cosen Corbet kindely. I heare his

---

[1] Daughter.   [2] i.e. their own people, relations.
[3] i.e. scholastic exercises or examinations at Oxford.

broother goos alonge with the kinge to Yorke, which he
dous, becaus he estemes it to be the gallentry of a yonge
man.   I sent you the last weake a list of thos shoulders,[1]
which they say must goo with the kinge. . . . You forget
to rwit to Mr. Gower; he has had 4 fitts.   Mr. Simons tooke
your letter very kindely.   I must needs say, I neuer had
any maide that profest more respect to you than Mary
Barton, and I beleeue it is in truth; for shee is her fathers
daughter and can not disembell.   I finde her as good a
saruant as euer I had; if I coould but put a littell water in
her wine, and make her temper her hastiness! yet I cannot
say that euer shee gaue me any ill word.——my deare Ned,
the Lord blles you.

Your most affectinat mother,

BRILLIANA HARLEY.

The Letters of Lady Brilliana Harley.

From LADY BRILLIANA HARLEY,

To her son, EDWARD

Bucks and Herefordshire.   *2nd Nov.* 1638.

Good Need—I was dublly glad to reseaue your letter,
both for the asshureanc of your comeing weell to Oxford,
and that I reseued it by your fathers hand, whoo, I thanke
God, came well home yesterday, aboute foore a cloke.   I
am glad you like Oxford; it is true it is to be liked, and
happy are we, when we like both places and condistions
that we must be in.   If we could be so wise, we should finde
much more swetness in our lifes then we do: for sartainely
theare is some good in all condistions (but that of sinn),
if we had the arte to distract the sweet and leaue the rest.

<hr>

[1] Soldiers.

Nowe I ernestly desire you may haue that wisdome, that from all the flowers of learneing you may drawe the hunny and leaufe the rest. I am glad you finde any that are good, wheare you are. I belleue that theare are but feawe nobellmens sonne in Oxford; for now, for the most part, they send theaire [1] sonnes into France, when they are very yonge, theaire [2] to be breed. Send me word wheather my brother Bray doo send to you, and wheather Sr Robert Tracy did come to see you, for he toold your father he would; and let me knowe howe [3] sheawes you any kindenes, when you haue a fitte opertuenity. . . .

Your most affectinat mother till death,

BRILLIANA HARLEY.

Be carefull to keepe the Sabath.

The Letters of Lady Brilliana Harley.

From LADY BRILLIANA HARLEY,

to her son, EDWARD

Bucks and Herefordshire.   21*st May* 1641.

. . . Deare Ned, I could wisch your chamber weare in Linconsine [4] and not in the laine ouer against it; those lains weare the vnsweatests places in Loundoun, and allways the siknes [5] is in thos placess. I could wisch you had rather bine in the Tempell or Graseine.[6] Grasein mythinkes is a fine place. I would haue you tell your father what I thinke of your chamber and the howes. I would haue write to him about it meself, but that I thought it might trubell him to reade so longe a letter. I longe to heare how you are prouided for a man, and whoo shall

---

[1] Their.   [2] There.   [3] Who.
[4] Lincoln's Inn.   [5] The plague.   [6] Gray's Inn.

mainetaine Gorge at Oxford; for I heare he has not write
to his father aboute it this mornig.   Merredifes [1] hows that
Mr. Simons liued in fell on firer, but thankes be to God,
theare was not much hurt doun, only the walls of the
kichen burnt and pulled doune; the loos is thought to be
about 3l.   Mr. Ballam is fallen sike againe; he is no ouer
wise man.   I thanke God your brothers and sisters are
well.   The protestation [2] was taken on sabath day last
at Bromton, Wigmore and Lainterdine,[3] with much willing-
nes.   I desire to know wheather you tooke it.   I pray God
blles you, and giue you a comfortabell meeting with
your most affectinat mother,

BRILLIANA HARLEY.

I haue sent you a peace of angelica rooat [4]: you may
carry it in your pocket and bite some times of it.

The Letters of Lady Brilliana Harley.

From LADY BRILLIANA HARLEY,

To her son, EDWARD

Bucks and Herefordshire.   14*th Feb.* 1642.

My deare Ned—I am confident you longe to heare from
me, and I hope this will come to your hand, though it may
be it will be long first.   We are still threatned and iiniured
as much as my enimyes can poscibell.[5]   Theare is non that
beares part with me but Mr. Jams,[6] whoo has shouwed
himsellfe very honnest; none will looke towards Brompton,

---

[1] Meredith's.   [2] Taken by the House of Commons on 4th May.
[3] Leintwardine.   [4] A popular preventive against the plague.
[5] Lady Harley was besieged in her home, Brampton Brian Castle,
near Ludlow, by the Royalists.
[6] Mr. James.

but such as truely fears God; but our God still takes care of vs, and has exceedingly sheawed His power in presaruing vs. . . .

Now they [1] say, they will starue me out of my howes; they haue taken away all your fathers rents, and they say they will driue away the cattell, and then I shall haue nothing to liue vpon; for all theare ame is to enfors me to let thos men I haue goo, that then they might seas vpon my howes and cute our throughts [2] by a feawe rooges, and then say, they knewe not whoo did it; for so they say, they knewe not whoo draeue away the 6 coolts, but Mr. Connigsby keepes them, though I haue rwite to him for them. They haue vsed all means to leaue me haue no man in my howes, and tell me, that then I shall be safe; but I haue no caus to trust them. I thanke God we are all well. I long to see my cosen Hackellt.[3] I pray God blles you.

Your most affectinat mother,

BRILLIANA HARLEY.

The Letters of Lady Brilliana Harley.

From CARY VERNEY, LADY GARDINER,

To her brother, SIR RALPH VERNEY

Bucks and London.   1642.

Your letter wos very willcom, for last weeke wos the forst nues as i harde of the misfortin [4] you hav had amonst you so latly. all the hous at Coddisdone [5] and heare at Hill [6] knuit, bot thay ware all my frends so much as not tu tell me of it till thay hard the danger was ovar. I am hartyly glad you ar so well com hom: I pray god erge [7]

---

[1] The Royalist supporters in the district. [2] Throats. [3] Hackluyt.
[4] Smallpox. [5] Cuddesdon, where Cary went to live after her marriage. [6] In Bedfordshire. [7] ? protect, guide.

you, so pra take hede of bein to ventaros, and Deare
brother let mee entret you not tu be so ventaros as tu let
pore Mon [1] com hom. I am so frad of that child that i du
wis him heare with all my hart. brother, i du thanke you
for the care you have takin of my tronk, and am resolvede
it shall fare as yours dus. With many thanks, for this and
all other favors. . . . I heare the Kinge is comin up tu
London, and i am very glad att itt, for i shall hop tu see my
father ther, for i hope tu bee in London some part of this
winter, though wher tu bee i cannot it till.[2] My brother
and sister Pollmar [3] presents their sarvis to you and the
rest of the company.

The Verney Memoirs.

From CARY VERNEY, LADY GARDINER,
        To her brother, SIR RALPH VERNEY

Bucks and London.   28*th July* 1642.

I must let you know how wel I lik this place. I am
confident you do wiss me so wel ass to be glad of my
contentment. Except the lose of all your good companie
i have more than i did look for. Whin I came my gran-
mother bid me very wellcom and made what entertanement
shee cod, more a gret dele then I expeckted, and Sir tomas [4]
and my laydy bid mee very wellcom to Coddisdon and
sade they wisht it might bee my one, and truly uesis
mee very civilly. . . . All my sistars [5] with a grit dele of

---

[1] Sir Ralph Verney's eldest son.   [2] Yet say.   [3] Palmer, i.e. Cary's
brother-in-law and his wife.
[4] Sir Thomas Gardiner, her father-in-law.
[5] i.e. sisters-in-law.   This letter was written just after her marriage.
She was fifteen.

complimentes did bid mee very wellcom and truly for the contarry pleshar, wee have it, for we ar abrod every day tordis evening in the coche. . . . I hope I shall give no cos to bar myself of so grit a plesshur as contentment. Deare brother lit mee now have bot contentment more, that is, as to let mee heare how my father and yourselfe dus. Pray when that you wright to my father, present my ombel duty to him, and let him kno I am will.

The Verney Memoirs.

From LADY SYDENHAM,

To LADY VERNEY

London.   1642.

My hart, i ded as much long for your answer of min, becaus that you ded exspres a trobell in yours to me about your hosbands reselushons. My dere hart, now i hope that you ar resalefed [1] of what he will do, and that i finde is better to won,[2] thin to levef [3] betwen hopes and fars what will happen. i know he has chossen the strongest part,[4] but i cannot thinke the best, but i am confedent he dus beleve tis the best, and for that he chos it. But truly, my hart, it stagers me that he shold not se clerly all thar wayes, being it tis so aparrant, for how tis for the lebberty of the subget to tacke all from thim which ar not of thar mind, and to puld [5] don thar houses, and impresen thim, and levef [6] thim to the marsy of the unruly multetude—i cannot fined that this is the lebberty of the subgete. Nor

---

[1] Resolved.   [2] One.   [3] Live.

[4] i.e. the Parliamentarian cause. Sir Ralph, Lady Verney's husband, fought for Parliament while his father, Sir Edmund, fought for the king.

[5] Pull.   [6] Leave.

do i find that it is in god's lay [1] to tacke arms aganst thar laful king to depos him, for shuer thay havef not mad his parrsen knon to all thos that thay havef implyed in this war to spare him and not to kill him.   But i trost god will protecket him, and my dere, if any of my frinds fall in this quarill i trost thar soles will be happy, for shuer tis laful to fitt [2] for won's laful king.

The Verney Memoirs.

From Ralph Josselin's [3] *Diary*

Earls Colne (Essex).   1644.

Sept. 3rd. Visited a sicke man one Guy Penhacke who was much troubled in mind upon his life: he had strong temptacons from Sathan.   I urged him to a Covent [4] with God to bee a new man if he recovered. . . .

Sept. 5. Stung I was with a bee on my nose, I presently pluckt out ye sting, & layd on honey, so that my face swelled not; thus divine providence reaches to the lowest things.   Lett not sin, oh Lord, that dreadful sting, bee able to poyson mee. . . .

Sept. 17. My good ffreind, Mr. Harlakenden sold one bagge of hops for mee, wherin I was advantaged 1l. 15s. This was Gods good providence. . . .

Oct. 1. I rid to Wethersfeild, injoyed the company of good freinds, saw some manuscripts of things in K. James & Charles his time of consequence; I had yr [5] a good bargaine of bookes.

Oct. 3. I payd 4s. excise for 2 bagges of hoppes; much

---

[1] Law.   [2] Fight.
[3] Vicar of Earls Colne, 1640-83.
[4] 'Covenant,' promise.   [5] There.

love in my freinds the Commissioners who payd my ordinary [1] for mee. . . .

Jan 17 [1644/5]. This day one of the butchers brought mee in a quarter of mutton, told not who sent it but went his way. I shall inquire whose love it was, & be thankfull for y[e] same. He that gives to the poore lends to y[e] L[d]. I have often observed my liberality, or rather my poore mite, imployed for y[e] publike, or upon others indigent, hath returned in with gaine and advantage. I must observe y[e] weeke: on mooneday I sent to my poore Sister 3s., & some other small things to others not worth y[e] mentioning; now y[s] [2] weeke I received 9l. from S[r] John Jacob which was in part due long before, and promised but was not payd untill now; divers invitacons of freinds to y[r] [3] houses: one sends me a parcel of plums & sugar, another a quarter of good mutton, another a fatt goose, another a capon and cheese, an unexpected income of a summ of mony layd out before; God good to my family & nacon.[4]

From *The Autobiography of Anne, Lady Halkett* [5]

c. 1656.

As soone as his [6] health would allow of travaile, wee tooke journy and came to N. Castle,[7] where I was so obleigingly intertained by S[r] Ch. and his lady, and with so much

[1] The public meal regularly provided at a certain fixed price at taverns and inns.

[2] This.   [3] Their.   [4] Race, 'stock.'

[5] Anne Murray, daughter of Thomas Murray, secretary to Prince Charles (Charles I), married Sir James Halkett, 1656.

[6] The infant son of Sir Charles Howard.

[7] Naworth Castle.

respect from the whole familly, that I could nott butt
thinke my selfe very hapy in so good a societty, for they
had an excellent governed familly having great affection
for one another; all there [1] servantts civill and orderly;
had an excellent preacher for there chaplaine, who preached
twice every Sunday in yᵉ chapell, and dayly prayers morning and evening. Hee was a man of a good life, good
conversation, and had in such veneration by all as if hee
had beene there tutelar angell. Thus we lived sometime
together, with so much peace and harmony as I thought
nothing could have given an interruption to itt. Butt itt
was too great to last long, for the post (going by weekely)
one day brought mee sad letters; one from C. B. [2] giving
mee accountt that just the night before hee intended to
come North, having prepared all things for accomplishing
what we had designed, hee was taken and secured in the
Gate-house att Westminster, and could expect nothing
butt death. With much dificulty hee had gott that con-
veyed outt to mee to lett me know what condittion hee was
in, and that he expected my prayers, since nothing els I
could doe could be avealable. . . . Presently affter I
receaved a letter from my brother M. [3] and another from
my sister N., [4] his very seveare, hers more compasionate,
but both representing C. B. under yᵉ caracter of the most
unworthy person living; that hee had abused mee in pre-
tending his wife was dead, for shee was alive; and that her
unckle Sir Ralph S. [5] had assured them both of itt, wᶜʰ
made nott only them butt all that ever had kindnese for
mee so abhorre him, that though he were now likely to dye,
yett none pittyed him. Had the news of either of these

[1] Their.

[2] Colonel Bamfield, suitor to Anne before her marriage.

[3] Murray. [4] Newton. [5] Perhaps Sir Ralph Shafto of Benwill.

K

come singly itt had beene enough to h⌄ve tryed the strengh of all the relligion and vertue I had, butt so to bee surrounded with misfortunes conquered what ever could resist them, and I fell so extreamely sicke that none expected life for mee.

From H. C.,

    To GIDEON HAYDON

Cornwall.   *9th Jan.* 1656.

Good Brother,—By my sister Tamsen [1] I herd of the welfare of you and my good sister, with the reste of your Frinds and family; to all in perticuller [2] I intreat my moste harty dues. We all have in these parts, my Father and myselfe in particuler, made our appearance to the Lord Desburoes [3] summons this day. . . .

Any that have ben againste my L[d]. Protecter or his government since 1653, their estates to be sequestred, 1 yard lefte for their wife and children, and they themselves imprisoned or sent beyond seas. Any that shoes [4] a disafection in words are subject to sequestration. If a man have £20 old rent, they doe comonly vallew it att six times so much, which amounts it to £120 per ann.; if he have an estate in pressant for his wife's life, he shall pay as if it weare his one [5]; or if it be his wife's.

No minester or scoller elected out of college or parsonage is to be kept in a man's house, or to teach his children, on paine of double his fine. . . .

I suppose this is bad newes enough, which doth much

---

[1] ? Thomasin(e), Thompson.   [2] Individually.

[3] John Desborough, one of the twelve major-generals.

[4] Shows.   [5] Own.

aflicte and trouble abundance of poore gents, and indeed there is a will to doe what there pleasuer [1] is further with home they pleasse. God give all humble harts and patience. . . . I am now goinge for Ierland again, wher I shall speand sume of this sumer, by God's assistance, hoopinge for a more fredom ther. S[r] I shall ever be your poore obleged Brother to serve you.

H. C.

The Trevelyan Papers.

From MARGARET VERNEY, LADY ELMES,
      To her brother, SIR RALPH VERNEY

Bucks and London.   *4th June* 1665.

The first inst we arived att the nasty Spaw,[2] and have now began to drinke the horid sulfer watter, which all thowgh as bad as is posable to be imajaned, yet in my judgment plesant to all the doings we have within doorse, the house and all that is in it being horidly nasty and crowded up with all sorte of company, which we Eate with in a roome as the spiders are redy to drope into my mouthe, and sure hathe nethor been well cleaned nor ared this doseuen yerese, it makes me much moare sicke then the nasty water. Did you but see me you wolde laughe hartily att me, but I say little of it to whot I thinke; then to mend all this, the goe to supper att halfe an ower after six, soe I save a bitt and supp bye myselfe 2 owers after them, which is the plesantest thinge I doe heare. We are 16 of my uncle and aunts family, and all in pention,[3] att

---

[1] Their pleasure.
[2] Knaresborough, Yorks. Lady Elmes had gone there to escape the plague.   [3] *En pension.*

10s. a weeke for owerselves, and 7s. for owr servants with lodgens in; I have not hard from you I know not when, soe in my openyone live heare as if theare ware nobody Elce in the worlde, but just whot I see of these bumkins. We met the Lady Comton and her sister the Lady Ann Comton att Donkister, hoe asured me the blackimorse head [1] in Chancery laine was shutt up of the plaige.

The Verney Memoirs.

From LADY HOBART,

To SIR RALPH VERNEY

London.   *3rd Sept.* 1666.

O dear Sir Raph,—I am sory to be the mesinger of so dismall news, for por London is almost burnt down. It began on Saterday night, & has burnt ever senc and is at this tim more fears then ever; it did begin in pudding lan at a backers, whar a Duch rog lay, & burnt to the bridge & all fish street and all crasus stret,[2] & Lumber Stret and the old exchang & canans stret & so all that way to the reaver and bilingsgat sid, & now tis com to chep sid and banescasell,[3] & tis thought flet stret will be burnt by tomorow, thar is nothing left in any hous thar, nor in the Tempell, thar was never so sad a sight, nor so dolefull a cry hard, my hart is not abell to expres the tenth nay the thousenth part of it, thar is all the carts within ten mils round, & cars & drays run about night and day, & thousens of men & women carring burdens. Tis the Duch fire, thar was one tacken in Westminster seting his outhous on fier & thay have atempted to fier many plases & thar is a bundanc tacken with granades & pouder. Casell yard was

[1] The Blackamoor's Head.
[2] Gracious Street, old name of Gracechurch Street.
[3] Baynard's Castle, east of Blackfriars Bridge.

set on fier, I am all most out of my wits, we have packed
up all our goods & cannot get a cart for money, thay give
5 & 10 pound for carts. . . .

God bles us & send us a good meting, & beleve I am yours
for ever,

A. H.

September the 3 ten aclock.

The Verney Memoirs.

From CARY VERNEY, LADY GARDINER,

To her brother, SIR RALPH VERNEY

Bucks and London.   *4th May* 1674.

I should bee more contented if his daughter Ursula [1]
ware not heare, who after 8 months plesure came homb
unsatisfied, declaring Preshaw was never so irksome to her,
& now hath bin at all the Salsbury rasis, dancing like wild
with Mr. Clarks whom Jack can give you a carictor of, &
came home of a Saturday night just before our Winton
rasis, at neer 12 a clok when my famyly was a bed, with
Mr. Charls Torner, a man I know not, Judg Torner's son,
who was tryed for his life last November for killing a man,
one of the numbar that stils themselves Tiborn Club, And
Mr. Clarks brother, who sat up 2 nights till neer 3 a Clok,
& said shee had never bin in bed sinc shee went a way till
4 in the morning, & danced some nights till 7 in the Morning.
Then shee borrowed a coach & went to our rasis, & wod
have got dancars if shee could, then brought homb this
crue with her a gaine, & sat up the same time. All this
has sophytiently vexed me . . . & Fryday shee was
brought home & brought with her Mr. Torner's linin to be

[1] i.e. her stepdaughter, Ursula Stewkely, daughter of John
Stewkely, of Preshaw, Cary's second husband.

mended & washed heare & sent after him to London,
where he went on Saturday, to see how his brother Mun
is come of his tryall for killing a man just before the last
sircut, And sinc these ware gone, I reflecting on thes
actions & shee declaring she could not be pleased without
dancing 12 hours in the 24, & takeing it ill I denied in my
husband's absenc to have 7 ranting fellows come to Preshaw
& bring musick, was very angry, & had [1] ordered wher they
should all ly,[2] shee designed mee to ly with Peg G., & I
scaring her & contrydicting her, we had a great quorill.

The Verney Memoirs.

From CARY VERNEY, LADY GARDINER,[3]
To her brother, SIR RALPH VERNEY

Bucks and London.   10th *March* 1685/6.

You are very sevear, and I cannot bot say unjust to
Accus mee of Whot you due not know to bee truth, and of
whot I can truly take my oath is falc, and yr Informars
divilish lyars that tell you I have bin such a lusar at play.
I know the originall of all the ill is said of mee; thay goe
about the earth sekking to mischef me. . . . A Church
farissy and an hypocrit may easily ruing any under my
sircomstances, but as low as I am, I scorn them and all
thay can due to mee & wod not goe ovar the thrashold
to satisfy yr Informars that has bin so long hatching
this mischef. . . . Whot quollyfications A gaimster should

---

[1] i.e. Ursula had.   [2] Sleep.

[3] Lady Gardiner had taken to gambling at cards in her later life.
She had written to Sir Ralph for the loan of £100, and had received
in reply a sermon and a promise of the £100 if she would give up
playing. This is her reply, which Sir Ralph described in his next as
'sharpe as a Dagger whetted for execution.'

have I am A strangare to, bot whot dus becom A gentil-
woman as plays only for divartion I hope I know, and shall
nevar due no base thing at play, nor no othar way. For
my high play, I am sure when I play with thos as is of great
quollyty, there is fore of us joyn as one gang, wch is much
loware to my shar than whot I used to play at my cossen
Nicholasis, and I nevar played at My Lady Deavonshirs
bot thre times, and then my Lady Seamore and my Lady
met, and Mrs. Vernon went equall shars with me. . . .
Tis true I play with my Lady Fits, bot wee often have
sherars, tho I am so Insincsible A creture yet I know did I
find gameing had bin so prediditiall I had long sinc left it,
and why you should injoin me to leve play quite I think is
hard, and as hard as I should not visit, sartainly that cannot
ruing mee. I know my erour and wher I have out lived
myselfe, and that is in hous keeping, and that I confes and
will Amend, and thank you for yr advise tho it extends to
a high severyty.

The Verney Memoirs.

From EDMUND VERNEY,

    To his son, EDMUND, at Oxford University

Bucks and London.   *6th July* 1686.

Child—I heard that the players are gon down to Oxford,
but I am unwilling that you should go to see them act, for
fear on your coming out of the hot play house into the
cold ayer, you should catch harm, for as I did once coming
out of the Theatre at a publick Act when it was very full
and stiaminghot and walkin a Broad in the cold, and gave
me sutch a cold that it had Likt to a cost me my Life.
Your best way in Sutch a cold is to go hom to your one[1]
chamber directly from the play house, and drink a glass of

[1] Own.

Sack, therefour Be sure you send your Servant At your hand for a bottle of the Best Canary and Keep it in your chamber for that purpose. Be sure you drink no Kooleing tankord nor no Cooling drinks what so ever.—harkon Thou unto the voyce & advise of mee Thy ffather, Loving Thee Better then him selfe.

EDMUND VERNEY.
The Verney Memoirs.

From ALICE HATTON,
To her brother, LORD HATTON

Northants and London.   *3rd Feb.* 1687.

You had heard from me last post, dearest Brother, but by a misstake my letter was forgott to be sent, wch I fretted extreamely att, but was born for misfortune of all kinds, and I am sure it would be ye greatest to me in ye world to give y^r L^{dp} the least occation to beleeve y^t any thing can ever make me omite paying all the duty and respect that is due to ye best of brothers. . . .

Captain Hatton [1] has had an unfortunait accident hapnd at Carlile. I have not heard a perfect relation how ye quarrell began, but in short, Livetenant Gorge Comley [2] has killed Majoer Morgan . . . and tis said nobody was by when it was don but Captain H. There are two papist offisers put into theire places.

Lady Manchester and all ye young ladies very well, present theere servis to y^r L^{dp} and my deare sister. She is this day gone to a weding feast. Ld Colrain's son married to a marchants daughter in ye citty. . . . The death of ye lettl Princess,[3] Lady Anne, is a great aflection to y^e

[1] Charles Hatton, brother of Lord Hatton.
[2] A lieutenant of Charles Hatton's company.
[3] Anne Sophia, daughter of the Princess Anne, born 1686.

Princes.[1] . . . The Dean of Paul's [2] presents his servis to y^r L^{dp}. I find he is very well enclined to leave St. Andrews, but soe many parswades him against it, he is not yet resolved w^t to doe. . . . It seems La.[3] North was conserned in making ye match for Mr. Spencer. She invited them both to her house, and when they met she locked them in a rome together. There are many surcomstances too long to trouble your L^{dp} wth, from, my dearest Brother,

Y^r most truly af^{et} [4] sister and

most obedient servant,

A. H.

The Hatton Correspondence.

From THE COUNTESS OF NOTTINGHAM,

To her father, LORD HATTON

Northants and London.   *3rd July* 1690.

My Lord [5] has at this present so little time to himself, he hopes your Lord^{sp} will pardon his not writting to you. . . .

We are all in twone [6] full of what concerns the fleet,[7] upon wch account my Lord Torrington is very hardly [8] spoke of, whither [9] diservedly or no, I must have a better insight to sea fight then I have at this distance to, to venter [10] to judge whither he deserves it or no; but wone [11] thing is certaine, y^t, after the engagement was begun, he let all lye upon the Dutch squadron, and did not engage at all wth the French fleet, wch squadron had certainly been quite lost, but y^t the Duke of Grafton, who in this expedi-

---

[1] Princess (Anne).
[2] Edward Stillingfleet, made Bishop of Worcester, 1689.
[3] Lady.   [4] Affectionate.
[5] Her husband, Lord Nottingham.   [6] Town, London.
[7] The Battle of Beachy Head, 30th June 1690.
[8] Harshly.   [9] Whether.   [10] Venture.   [11] One.

tion has got immortal fame, would fight, and wone ship
more came to there [1] assistance. . . . There is a report y^t
six ships of the French are disabled, and y^t they are toing [2]
them towards some of there owne ports, and y^t the Plimouth
squardon is gone after them.   My Lord Stweard [3] and
my Lord Pembroke [4] have been so brave to offer their
service to the Queene, and are gone downe to Dover. I
suppose my Lord Pembroke will command his owne Marine
regiment, and my Lord Stwart [3] will either be a volontier
or have some command.

It is past ten a clock.   I am afraid the post will be gone.
I am y^r Los^p. most obedient daughter,

A. NOTTINGHAM.
The Hatton Correspondence.

From ELIZABETH HATTON,

To her brother-in-law, LORD HATTON

Northants and London.   *3rd July* 1690.

I received y^r Ld^pps kind letter, wch at this present time I
doe much want.   I could wish I wase able to give y^r
Ld^pps a true account of what Mr. Hatton [5] is acused of,
but I am very ignorant, for I did not in ye least know of
anything tell [6] ye messenger came for him, and then I had
not time to inquire of him, and I cannot larne [7] of any
person that have seen it what is in it, but most doe say
there is nothing in that can tuch [8] his life.   I trust in God
tis true. . . . I have don all I can in ye world to get leave
to goe into ye Tower, tho I am willing to be a close prisenor [9];

[1] Their, the Dutch.   [2] Towing.
[3] The Earl of Devonshire.   [4] First Lord of the Admiralty.
[5] Her husband, Charles Hatton, brother of Lord Hatton, confined
in the Tower on charge of writing a libellous pamphlet.
[6] Until.   [7] Learn.
[8] Touch, endanger.   [9] i.e. be imprisoned with him.

for he hath noebody wth him, and should he be sick it may prove of a very ill consequence. . . . I beg of y^r Ld^{pps} to writ to ye President that he may have ye liberty of ye Tower, and that he may be aloud [1] that sumtimes he may see his frends, or those persons wch he hath reall business wth concerning his one [2] affairs.   And allsoe I humble [3] beg y^r Ld^{pps} will be pleased to writ to som of ye Privi Counsell, that I may have order to goe into ye Tower, for I will asure y^r Ld^{pps} I am under soe much sorrow that tis impossibell to be exprest, or can I support myself, for I can declare I have sleept not one houre in a night sence he hath ben there.   I have another favor to desire of y^r Ld^{pps}, that y^u would be pleased to consider his condition, and that ye place is very chargeable,[4] and noe person that he doe owe but sixpence to but is pressing and rude, wch makes me exposed daly [5] to great inconveniencys. . . .

I am y^r Ld^{pps} most faithfull, humble servent,

E. HATTON.

The Hatton Correspondence.

From CARY VERNEY, LADY GARDINER,
To her brother, SIR RALPH VERNEY
Bucks and London.   *18th and 20th June* 1693.

Deare Brother, — Isterday Mr. Keeling brought y^r grandaughter [6] to mee, wch I confes was the sadest meeting

---

[1] Allowed.   [2] Own.   [3] Humbly.   [4] Expensive.   [5] Daily.
[6] Molly Verney, aged about fifteen, was to have married a Mr. Dormer, but took the matter into her own hands and disappeared from her uncle John's house, leaving a note to the effect that she was already married to a Mr. Keeling, a gentleman with plenty of aristocratic relations, but no money. Molly was Edmund's daughter, and had lost both her father and brothers by this time. Her mother, who lived till she was seventy-four, was insane.

I ever had with her, & maid my children stand like mutes
being so full of grife.   Bot I told my mind to him fust; & at
last took corage to spake to her wch I find is highly afflicted
for offending you & begs you will give her leve to beg her
pardon on her knees of you for marying without y^r consent. .

My Lady Rossel told me isterday that my Lord Soffolks
daughter was lately marryed much wors, for she has
marryed A vally de shamber. . . .

The Verney Memoirs.

From CHARLES HATTON,

To his brother, LORD HATTON

Northants and London.   17*th Dec.* 1698 *and* 30*th Dec.* 1699.

I sent you by ye carier last Thursday ye History of
Quiestisme,[1] but it is only borrowed of a French gentleman.
I cou'd not buy it at any of ye booksellers.   When you have
done wth it, pray return it.   I didnt heare, nor cannot be
enform'd y^t Madam Dacier translated Florus.[2]   I am very
well acquainted wth her brother Tanaquil le Fevre, who
hath been severall times at my house; and he told me he
lodg'd in Suffolk street, 'vis à vis le Livrre Rouge,' but his
Red Book proved to be ye Roe Buck. . . .

30*th Dec.* 1699.

Yesterday an acquaintance of mine came to see me and
did much divert me wth some stories he told of Sr Francis
Compton,[3] y^r old acquaintance, his fondness of his new
virtuous and pious lady.   The day before, Sr Francis came
into company wher my friend was; he told them his lady

[1] *Dilaogues Posthumes du Sieur de la Bruyere sur le Quietisme* is
the book referred to.

[2] Her work was *L. A. Flori rerum Romanarum Epitome*, Paris, 1674.

[3] Who had had many wives.

was so very devout, she was every day severall hours in her closet at her prayers.   And he having then seen her take up her bible and prayer booke, and go into her closet, he was assur'd she wou'd be ther shut up for severall houres. In y[e] meane time he came abroad to divert himself wth taking a glasse of wine.   Presently after w[ch], my friend going to y[e] playhouse, he was fully convinc'd my Lady Compton did not make so long prayers as S[r] Francis reported, for he found her in a vizard and maske in y[e] 18[d] gallery.

C. HATTON.

The Hatton Correspondence.

From ALICE HATTON [1]

To her father, LORD HATTON

Northants and London.   *Sept.* 1699.

My Lord, I am so overjoy'd when I hear from y[r] Lord[sp], its not to be express'd.   I desire you will beg pardon for me to my Lady for writting such a short letter to her, and tell her I was last night at St. Jeames, and y[t] ther was but a few dancers.   Y[e] best were Lady Hartington,[2] Lady Betty Candish,[3] Mrs. Lutteril, Mrs. Godfrey and Lady Essex, and Mrs. Roper who was y[e] new dancer.   Indeed she did it very well, but had too much indeavour'd to imitat Lady Hartingtons noding her head, w[ch] is only becomeing to herself. Y[e] best of y[e] men was Lord Antrim, Lord Anglese,[4] and Lord Essex.   But my Lord Antrim has cut his hear,[5]

---

[1] Lord Hatton's daughter by his second marriage.

[2] Wife of William Cavendish, Lord Hartington, afterwards second Duke of Devonshire.

[3] Daughter of the first Duke of Devonshire.

[4] Lord Anglesey.   [5] Hair.

and got one of ye new fassioned perewks,[1] w[ch] have so much hear in them y[t] a good one cant cost les than 60 pound, and y[t] monstros bignes wth his lettle face did not look so well. . . .

My Aunt Portman [2] desires you to write to my Aunt Mary, to bie [3] her a set of y[e] French baskets they use for a desert,[4] and y[e] couler [5] are to be white and gold and grean, and when you get hers Nevil desires a set too, and if you will take care to bay [6] my Aunt Mary for them, and they'l bay you again.   My Aunt sayes y[t] if you will give me leave to learn to draw, Mrs. Tollett shall teach me.   I desire my duty to my Lady, and service to all my friends at Kirby.

I am, my Lord,

Yr dutyfull daughter,

A. E. H.

The Hatton Correspondence.

From CHARLES HATTON,

To his brother, LORD HATTON

Northants and London.   28th Sept. 1699 *and* 21*st May* 1700.

. . . I shall endeavour to procure you from Paris some acorns of ye Ilexs [7] you desire.   Mr. Evelyn hath been wth me, and tells me he hath a new booke of sallating [8] just finish'd at y[e] press, and will be publish'd y[e] next week. He setts up for a great virtuoso in sallating.   In his booke he takes notice y[t] juice of oranges in salats is preferable to

[1] New-fashioned perukes.

[2] Wife of Sir Henry Seymour Portman, and sister to Lord Hatton's third wife.

[3] Buy.   [4] Dessert.   [5] Colour.   [6] Pay.   [7] Ilex.

[8] *Acetaria, or a discourse of Sallets*, London, 1699; 'sallating,' making of salads.

vinegar. But ye oranges must be cut with a silver knife, for a steele blade will give a tincture of steele to ye juice. . . .

21st May 1700.

It is reported y^t ye B^p of Durham [1] is maryed to one M^{ls} Offley. Her uncle was groome-porter, her father a parson, and her brother is a parson. She had 2 sisters marryed to parsonns; one of y^m [2] (who is dead) to ye Deane of Carlisle. Whilst his wife was alive and at Durham, where he is Prebendary, she and her mother (it is thought) by their interest wth ye B^p, prevai'd wth him to marry his last lady, and, ever sinc, ye mother hath improv'd her interest so as to pervayle wth ye B^p to marry her daughter, who is about 40 yeares of age, not handsome, and hath been long known by ye name of Duck-leggs. The match is assuredly concluded betwixt Dr. Burnet and ye widow Berkley,[3] of Worcestershire, who was Sr Ric^d Blages [4] daughter. I am

Y^r Lo^{pps} very humble servant,

C. HATTON.

The Hatton Correspondence.

From LADY WENTWORTH [5]

To her son, LORD RABY (EARL OF STRAFFORD)

Yorks and London.   18*th Sept.* 1705.

My dearist dear and best of children, I am much rejoysed at your fyne present, I wish you may often have such and

---

[1] Lord Crewe; but he did not marry Mistress Offley.   [2] Them.

[3] i.e. widow of Robert Berkeley of Spetchley.

[4] Sir Richard Blake's.

[5] Sometime Lady of the Bedchamber to James II's queen. She was between fifty and sixty at the time of writing these letters.

better, tell you ar as ritch as the Duke of Molberry [1] whoe
is billding the fynest hous at Woodstock that ever was
seen; thear is threscore rooms of a flower, noe stairs, only
a little pair that goes to the uper rooms, which ar only for
sarvents, and staitly wood, which he cutts out walks in,
and fyne gardens that are fower myles about. It is
beleeved furneture and al cannot cost les than three hundred
thoussand pd, the house will cost above a hundred thousand
pd. Why should you not be as fortunate as he? . . .

I hard a strang od story the other day of Lord Bradford,
you know thear is Prayers at Twitnam [2] wensdays and
frydays. Sir William Humble was Buiryed either of
Satterday or sunday and the scutyons [3] was upon the
reeding desk, and the wensday following, after prayers was
up, Lord Bradford toar them down, and stampt them under
his feet. Lady Humble's Aunt was thear, and told him his
devotion was great that could put himself into soe unusyell
a pation, without any provocation; and Mr. Lastrang [4]
told him this was what did not becom a man of his age,
honor, and Quallety. My Lord sternly askt him whoe he
was, he told him he was a gentleman. Sum say it put him
in mynd of death, and that was what vext him, others say
it was sumthing in the arms that offended him, thear being
more in them then did belong to Sir Willyam, and others
that they should not have hung there soe long. This is as
Mrs. Isbell tells me: All our dums [5] ar well, Pug [6] and
Fubs [7] ar the pretiest of thear kynde, sure. . . .

The Wentworth Papers.

[1] The Duke of Marlborough.   [2] Twickenham.
[3] Scutcheons.   [4] Lestrange.   [5] i.e. dumb creatures, pets.
[6] Her monkey.   [7] Her dog.

From LADY WENTWORTH,

To her son, LORD RABY (EARL OF STRAFFORD)

Yorks and London.   13*th Jan.* 1706.

. . . I have hard you say you have been aquanted with my Lord Carbury [1]; his daughter, you know, was to have Lord Shrosbery [2] whoe you know is maryed to an Etalyon.[3] This lord's daughter is about seventeen, exstreemly good, and very handsom, and very modist and vertuously brought up, millions better then our great cosen W.[4]   Write Lord Carburer word, you ar desperet in lov with his daughter, and that mony he wants not, and that you will make as good a husband as Lord Shrosberry.   I have hard of spels I wish I could giv that lord one, that he might be as desierus to have you his sun in law as I am of having it soe.   Mrs. W.[5] was att the parlement hous the other day, I thinck she sett up her fyne coach and ekopadg [6] before you went, which moste lauhgs at; and between you and I she is not much admiered, and is not thought discreet in her carridg. This is only between freinds,[7] of which you are that pretious jewell to me, which Solloman ses, and is sartainly soe hard to be found, but highly to be vallyed [8] when found, and non can be more then you ar by, etc.

The Wentworth Papers.

---

[1] Carbery.   His daughter referred to here married the Marquis of Winchester.

[2] Shrewsbury.   [3] Italian.

[4] Thomas Wentworth, formerly Thomas Watson, second son of Lord Rockingham and nephew of Sir William Wentworth, who left him the bulk of his estate.   He changed his name to Wentworth, and was therefore disliked by his relations to whom had been left the empty title only.

[5] Presumably Mrs. Wentworth, his wife.   [6] Equipage.

[7] Put here in the old sense of *kin, relatives.*   [8] Valued.

L

From ANN CECIL [1]

To LORD RABY (EARL OF STRAFFORD)

Yorks and London.   WAKEFIELD.   *4th Aug.* 1708.

My Lord,

It is with abundance of shame I give you this trobel to beg a faveor I haed not confidenc to aske on you when hear nor inded cane I now dow it with ouet blushin, it is my Lord to beg the faver on you to speak to my Lord Duek of Malbrow for my sone that hee will be pleased to give him a letill betor commison, he is bashfull and cannot speak for him self, if your Lordship goes for Flandors.   If not I beg the faver on you to wriet to the Duek in his be holfe. I know my Lord it is in your puer, ben [2] a genrall, and that the Duek won't refues aneything you aske.   My son joynes with me in begin this faver of you, and if you my Lord reqire it, he can have severall frends to give your Lordship an acount of his behaver which I hope won't be below the caracktor of on you ar pleas'd to think worth spekin for. I humbly beg on you not to deny me this reqest, for I know you deliet in dowing good, if to me it is to a helplous widow and the best sone in the world.   Good my Lord don't deny, and I hope it may puet both him and me ouet of the necesity of givein you father [3] trobel.   I am not unsencabel of the obligacions I have to your Lordship, and I out [4] not to be furthor trublsum to you, but it is natrall to adres our selefes to thos wee hope to met [5] with a return from.   I hop my Lord will ablig [6] me in this and not to be more trobelsum I conclued my self, my Loard, etc.

ANN CECILL.

The Wentworth Papers.

[1] Daughter of William Oglethorpe of Wakefield.   The son of whom she speaks was Captain, afterwards Colonel Cecil, later a notorious Jacobite agent.

[2] Being.   [3] Farther.   [4] Ought.   [5] Meet.   [6] Oblige.

From LADY WENTWORTH,

To her son, LORD RABY (EARL OF STRAFFORD)

Yorks and London.   16*th Nov.* 1708.

My dearist and best of children. . . .

I have a moste dismall story to tell you, God forgiv me for it.   I cannot help being more then I ought concerned. I shall never lov anything of that kynde a quarter so well again.   I had rether lost a hundred pd., nay all the rest of my doms I would have geven to have saved poor charming Fubs,[1] never poor wretch had a harder death.   As it leved soe it dyed, full of lov leening its head in my bosom, never offered to snap at any body in its horrid torter [2] but nussle its head to us and loock earnestly upon me and Sue, whoe cryed for thre days as if it had been for a childe or husband, . . . Sure of all its kynd thear never was such a one nor never can be, soe many good qualletys, soe much senc and good nature and cleenly and not one falt; but few human creeturs had more senc then that had. . . . I could write a quier of paper in her commendations.   I have buiryed her in this garden, and thear is a stoan layd at her head. . . . I leiv all news and the discription of the Princ [3] his buirying to your brother.[4]

The Wentworth Papers.

[1] Her favourite pet dog.   Lady Wentworth had five dogs, a monkey, and a parrot.

[2] Torture.

[3] Prince George of Denmark.

[4] Peter Wentworth, who was equerry to Prince George.

From LADY WENTWORTH,

To her son, LORD RABY (EARL OF STRAFFORD)

Yorks and London.   24*th Feb. and* 6*th March* 1710.

. . . Its said that Duke Schoombork's [1] son is to marry a daughter of the Duke of Ormons.[2]   Secheverel [3] is to be tryed next thursday; thear is very deferent openyon of him.   Westminster Hall is full of Scaffolds. . . .

6th March.

. . . Secheverell will make all the Ladys turn good huswivs, they goe att seven every mornin.   Your brother givs you a more exact account then I can, pray God send it ends well, for this comfution [4] seems to me to be lyke the begining of the lait troubles, I having laitly red Bakers Cronekles.   I rejouce [5] you are safe, thear will be plenty of soagars [6] now, for I hear thear is a great many of the mob in custety,[7] that are all to be sent for sogars.   Mrs. Lewis, Mrs. Loe's neice was last Friday to see me very fynly drest and very noble jewells one.[8]   She keeps a coach and six horssis and fower footmen, did keep six but she being very discreet desiered twoe might be put ofe, for soe many would but make them be envyed; indeed she was always a great favorett of myne.   All my fyer syde is in good health. . . .

The Wentworth Papers.

From LADY WENTWORTH,

To her son, LORD RABY (EARL OF STRAFFORD)

Yorks and London.   1*st Aug.* 1710.

. . . I had soe many thancks to giv you last post I had

---

[1] Schomberg's.   [2] Ormond's.

[3] Dr. Henry Sacheverell, impeached for preaching a sermon against the Whig government and principles in St. Paul's Cathedral, November 1709.

[4] Confusion.   [5] Rejoice.   [6] Soldiers.   [7] Custody.   [8] On.

not room to answear you about the coach.   Edwards the
man you left me was a very good coach man, and gave the
smothist fynist words in the world, but had many shufling
ways with him.   He when he gott a new gob,[1] he would
chang my horsis and giv me ver bad ons, and often his
horsis would be laim, and then I could not have it, and some
timse the coach would want mending, and be taken ofe the
wheels under pretenc of mending, when being taken of and
put one has been al that has been don to it; but he has
wanted the horsis; this I have been told is the only reson.
This man [2] is a very good coach; a better can not be, he
will have none of thees tricks; he keeps me three very good
horsis hear, in case any mischanc coms to one.   But my
coach has not so much eas as you thinck, for although I
stayde at hom when I had none, yet now I seldom mis
going out to take the air, or make some threvolves [3] pretenc
to goe about the streets. . . .   I hard hear that the Grand
Chamberlin [4] is dead, is it true, pray tell me?   He that
was to goe to Hanover I hear kist the Queen's hand to goe
next day, and instead of goeing to Hanover went to Heaven,
I hope, for he died the very next day. . . .   Next pew [5] to
me thear setts a young lady very genteel and very fair, but
I thinck farr from a buity, but its said she is kept by the
Duke of Molberry; his dutchis for all she is many years
older then this, yet she is ten timse handsomer. . . .

The Wentworth Papers.

From LADY STRAFFORD,

To her husband, LORD STRAFFORD

London.   ST. JAMES'S SQUARE.   *27th Nov.* 1711.

   . . . Next to you I believe Lady Wentworth loves me
better then any of her childaren.   I own I believe sister [6]

[1] Job.   [2] i.e. the new man.   [3] Frivolous.
[4] James Cresset.   [5] i.e. at church.   [6] i.e. sister-in-law.

Betty in her self wou'd be very good humour'd, but my
sister [1] Aurundell governs her as won wou'd a child, and she
is with her every day and they get som little od body or
othere to play at cards, and such a dirty place sure nobody
ever went into, and they eat jelly and drink Chockolet from
morning tell night. . . . I went last week to see our pick-
tures and I like them worse than ever I did, for he has made
a Dwarfe of you and a Giant of me, and he has not tooched
the dressing of them sence you went.   I made Capt. Powell
scold at hime to mend them, for they are nethere of them
like.   He is so ingaged with the Marlborough daughters
that he minds no body elce.   The world says Lady Har.
Rialton has latly been in Pickell for her sins, and Lady
Jersey in the same way; if they are as bad as the town says
they are, I wonder they are ever out of it.   I think Lady
North and Gray a very prity sort of woman; we went to the
opera togethere last Satturday, and she seem'd mightily
pleased at my carring [2] of her. . . . Capt. Powell tells me
he carrys this, but I don't believe him for he has set so many
days to goe and has not.   He dined yesterday at Lord
Privey Seales, he says he hug'd and kiss'd Mrs. Robinson
extremly; I don't know which party was the most to be
envyed in those imbraces. . . . I fear som part of this
you 'll hardly read for I have speelt it abominably, but you
must take it for better for worse as you have don me, and
to my dearest soul, adieu, yours for ever.

The Wentworth Papers.

From LADY STRAFFORD,
            To her husband, LORD STRAFFORD
London.   ST. JAMES'S SQUARE.   25*th March* 1712.
    . . . I hear the Duke of Argile makes the greatest
prodistations of friendshipe for you that ever was.   My

[1] Touched.   [2] Carrying, taking.

father is layd up with the gout: I believe I shall jumble my
guts out between this and Russell street, for since my
fathere has been ill I hav gon every day.   Here is a new
play which has taken extremly, call'd the distrest mothere.
I had not seen it tell last night for I don't much love
Traidys,[1] but I think it 's a very good won.   Lady Massam [2]
is very ill and her son is like to dye.   'Tis said the Duchesses
of Somerset and Shrewsbery is at great difference with won
anothere.   I still am told you are to be Master of the
Horse.   I wish the Queen would make me a Lady of the
Bedchamber.   I wonder Lady Scarborough keepes her
place, for Lord Scarborough oposes the Queen in everything
that 's in his power with all the voiolence in the world. . . .
I fancy by this time you 'll think I never intend to cease
tormenting you with my nonsense.   I fancy every letter
you have from me you find me out to have less witt than
you thought before; but you have won thing for your
comfort, which is, the less witt wemen has the better wives
they make, so according to that rule you are a most happy
man in your choise.   *The Wentworth Papers.*

From LADY ANNE WENTWORTH, LADY LUCY WENTWORTH,
    and LORD WENTWORTH,[3]
            To their father, LORD STRAFFORD
Yorks and London.   1724 *and* 1730.

                        STAINBROUGH,
Dear Papa,[4]   15*th Nov.* 1724.
    I was very glad to hear by your Lordship's letter to my
mama that you think I am improved in my writing.   I

------

[1] Tragedies.   [2] Lady Masham.
[3] Lady Anne, the eldest daughter, Lady Lucy, the second, and
Lord Wentworth, born *c.* 1722, the only son.   There was a third
daughter, Lady Harriet.
[4] Anne was about eleven at this time.

have had as good luck as ever at cribadg, and am now very far from a bankerupt.   I have sent you a ribus [1] of my own making, and tho' [it] is not a good, yet I hope it will divert you.   Mrs. Lawson and Mrs. Oglethorp gives their service to you.   Lord Wentworth and Lady Hariot gives their duty to your Lordship.

I am, etc.

17th Nov. 1724.

DEAR PAPPA,

I hope your Lordship will excuse this being the first that ever I write in my life and i hope you will come hither soon for the country is very dull without your good company pray give my duty to my grandmamma i am dear pappa

your

most affectionate and

most dutifull

Daughter,

LUCY WENTWORTH.

12th Dec. 1730.

Dear Papa,

I have no news to tell you but Mr[s]. Southwell is dead. Pray Papa, give my duty to Lord Bathirst and my service to Lady Bathirst.   Monswer [2] I beleve is gone to France for he sent for his Trink [3] to the king's arms, and was ready in a hackney coach and toke in [4] in to him and bid them drif

---

[1] Rebus.   [2] Monsieur.   [3] Trunk.   [4] ? for *it*.

a way to jerin crose.[1]   This Letter is of my one spilling.
I am Dear Papa,

> Your most affectionate
>
> and most dutifull son,
>
> WENTWORTH.
>
> *The Wentworth Papers.*

[1] Charing Cross.

INDEX OF SPELLINGS

INDEX OF SPELLINGS

153

B

Banissed: banished, 55
Barer: bearer, 111
Bargened, bargenyng: bar‑gained, bargaining, 43
Bartylmew: Bartholemew, 83, 85
Bassetours: ambassadors, 37
Bay: pay, 138
Beceach: beseech, 116
Beche: bitch, 63
Beeg: beg, 115
Beer: bear (*sb.*), 56
Beest: best, 116
Befoor: before, 108
Begin: begging, 142
Behaf, behalve: behalf, 24, 41
Behaver: behaviour, 142
Be holfe: behalf, 142
Behould: behold, 91
Be(i)n: being, 121, 142
Bellowes: billows, 97
Belowyde: beloved, 75
Beniuolent: benevolent, 81
Besinesse, besynes(se): busi‑ness, 28, 40, 48
Betwhene: between, 63
Bichopp: bishop, 71
Bisiche: beseech, 75
Biusnes: business, 115
Blackimorse: Blackamoor's, 128
Blages: Blake's, 139
Bloude, blud: blood, 97, 103
Blushin: blushing, 142
Bluw: blue, 93
Bogke: book, 58
Boith: both, 74
'Book': buck, 136
Boouckes: books, 114
Borood: borrowed, 110
Bosschope: bishop, 72
Both: bought, 44
Bould(e): bold, 106, 107
Bowthe: both, 76

Boyth(e): both, 61, 87, 93; bought, 87
Breed: bred (*p.p.*), 118
Bregys: Bruges, 58
Bride: breed, 103
Brohut: brought, 63
Broodyr, broother: brother, 59, 117
Browth: brought, 92
Bruyng: brewing, 66
Buiryed: buried, 140, 143
Buishopes: bishops, 109
Buity: beauty, 145
Bumkins: bumpkins, 128
Burgayne: Bourgogne, Bur‑gundy, 36
Burgonys: Bourgognes, Bur‑gundians, 36
Burth: birth, 55
Busshop(pe): bishop, 73, 74, 79
Bwt: but, 42, 76
By: be, 72; *by(n)* buy, 32, 43, 74
Bysschyp: bishop, 72

C

Caas: case, story, adventure, 55
Camptayne: captain, 34
Canapy: canopy, 83
Candish: Cavendish, 137
Caracktor, carictor: character, 129, 142
Carridg: carriage, 141
Case: cause, 113, 115
Caster: Caistor, 46
Cauntorbery: Canterbury, 85
Cawyrsame: Caversham, 45
Cebarbes: suburbs, 108
Cecions: sessions, 78
Certan: certain, 74
Cete, cety: city, 88, 108
Chale: shall, 39
Chamberlin: Chamberlain, 145
Chambrych: Cambridge, 70

Divartion: diversion, 131
Do: to, 68
Docthur: doctor, 93
Don(e): down, 61
Donkister: Doncaster, 128
Doone: done, 95
Doorse: doors, 127
Dorothe: Dorothy, 113
Dott: doth, 25
Dou, dow(ing): do(ing), 115, 142
Doun: done, 119
Doune: down, 119
Dous: does, 114, 117
Douter: daughter, 71
Douth: doubt, 115
Dowryng: during, 76
Dowt(h)er: daughter, 47, 92
Dowyr: Dover, 63
Doyst: dost, 89
Draeue: 'drave,' drove, 120
Draught-brygge: drawbridge, 34
Dreed: dread, 90
Drevyn: driven, 63
Drue, druw: drew, 89, 91
Du: due, 68
Duch: Dutch, 128
Dudcote: Didcot, 43
Dus: does, 121, 122, 131
Dutchis: Duchess, 145
Dyde: died, 36
Dydge: ditch, 52
Dys: dish, 26
Dysceste: deceased, 66
Dysse: dice, 86
Dystrowyd: destroyed, 69
Dystrowynge: destroying, 85
Dystryde: destroyed, 37
Dystyme: this time, 25

E

Eande: end, 107
Eilldest: eldest, 113

Eingland: England, 105, 106, 108
Ekopadg: equipage, 141
Elce: else, 128
Embassador: ambassador, 112
Enfo(u)rme(d): inform(ed), 27, 29, 40
Enquer: inquire, 46
Entertanement: entertainment, 121
Entierly: entirely, 24, 40
Eny: any, 28, 33
Es: ease, 25
Escwysed: excused, 71
Esse: ease, 25
Etalyon: Italian, 141
Etter: eater, 53
Evere: every, 88
Ewangelys: Evangels, Gospels, 37
Ewer: ever, 75
Ewsed: used, 113
Ew-tre: yew-tree, 52
Eyer: air, 80
Eyres: years, 110
Eyse: ease, 31
Extreamely: extremely, 126

F

Falc: false, 130
Fal(l)t(s): fault(s), 111, 116, 143, etc.
Farissy: Pharisee, 130
Fars : fears, 122
Fassioned: fashioned, 138
Faule: fall, 100
Faver(able): favour(able), 29, 142
Favered: favoured, 33
Fawlyn: fallen, 63
Fayder: father, 61
Fayer: fair (*adj.*), 78, (*sb.*) 83
Fears: fierce, 128

Gunes, gunns: guns, 51, 52
Gyff(e): give, 54
Gyffyn, given, 88, 92
Gyte: get, 46

3 (= [ʒ] and [þ]
ʒe: year, 67
ʒow: though, 25
ʒu, ʒw: you, 32
ʒyth: yet, 25

H

Hable: able, strong, 66
Haed: had, 142
Haith: hath, 73, 74
Hale: ale, 57
Hallthe: health, 57
Ham: themselves, 30; them, 31
Hane: Ann, 57
Hanffull: handful, hand-breadth, 50
Hard(e): heard, 88, 104, 120, 128, etc.
Harhoddes: heralds, 83
Harme: arm, 89
Hart: hurt, 96
Hart(s): heart(s), 53, etc.
Hartte: hearty, 72
Hatfilde: Hatfield (House), 84
Havef: have, 123
Havyn: having, 36
Haw(h)e: have, 60, 67
Hayd: had, 61
Healpe, help, 107
Hear(e): here, 106, 113, 127, etc.; hair, 137
Hearifort: Hereford, 114
Heer: hair, 56; *heer(e)* here, 40, 41
Heey: hay, 61
Hefe: if, 67
Hensse: whence, 72

Heny: any, 62
Her: hear, 24, 52
Herry: Harry, Henry, 50
Hes(e): his, 40; has, 61
Hett: eat, 63
Hevir, hewyr: ever, 63, 67
Heyff: hithe, 93
Heynd: end, 67
Heyr: here, 68
Hier: hear, 109
Higthnes: Highness, 84
Hire, hiryng: hear(ing), 26, 27
Hoder: other, 58, 62
Hoe: who, 128
Hole: whole, 29
Holesome: wholesome, 66
Holdyn: holding, 36
Homb: home, 129
Home: whom, 73, 127
Honeste: honesty, 66
Hoo: who, 73
Hoole: whole, 48, 111
Hoope: hope, 107
Hoopinge: hoping, 127
Hooste: host, 51
Hos: whose, 63, 67
Hosbon: husband, 24
Hough: how, 46
Houlde: hold, 91
Housallde: household, 49
Howe: who, 118
How(gh)t: out, 60, 63
Howllde: old, 60
Howr: our, 42, 63
Howsold: household, 54
Howyn: own, 42
Howys: house, 49
Hoys: whose, 48, 64
Humble, humely: humbly, 35, 75, 107, etc.
Hurlpole: whirlpool, 104
Hus: us, 63
Hw: how, 32
Hyde: heed, 45
Hys: is, 57, 75

I

Imagen, imajaned: imagine(d), 110, 127
Imbassador: ambassador, 68
Imbraced, imbraces: embraced, embraces, 91, 146
Implyed: employed, 123
Importannss: importance, 68
Impresen: imprison, 122
Indevors: endeavours, 110
Indosyd: endorsed, 41
Ineryte: inherit, 110
Inforttewin: 'un'-fortune, misfortune, 63
Ingaged: engaged, 146
Ing(e)lond(e): England, 36, 37, 38
Insincsible: insensible, 131
Interly: entirely, 67
Intertained: entertained, 124
Invahar: inveigher, 97
Ironyos: erroneous, 85
Is: his, 68; this, 69
Isterday: yesterday, 135
Istructeth: instructeth, 81
It: yet, 121
Iven: even, 98
I-wrethen: written (*p.p.*), 62

J

Jantilwomen: gentlewomen, 71
Jayn: Jane, 49
Jepardes, jepart: jeopardy (-ies), 24
Jerin crose: Charing Cross, 149
Jeyst: joist, 66
Joberde: jeopardy, 49

K

Kecheynge: catching, 86
Kichin: kitchen, 119

Kipe: keep, 97
Kno(n): know(n), 122, 123
Knuit: knew it, 120
Knwe: knew, 114
Knytt: knight, 72
Kwd: could, 32

L

Laboryd: laboureth (*imper.*), 62
Lade(s): lady (-ies), 88, 92
Laful: lawful, 123
Laim: lame, 145
Laine: lane, 118, 128
Lait(ly): late(ly), 144
Lamehith: Lambeth, 41
Larne: learn, 134
Late(n): let, 27, 32
Lawhe: laugh, 56
Lawhynges: laughings, laughter, 56
Lawlie: lowly, 75
Lay: law, 123
Laydy: lady, 121
Laynes: lines, 109
Lay(s)yr: leisure, 71
Laytter: latter, 61
Leasur: ? harm, injury, 102
Leatter: letter, 107,
Leaufe: leave (*sb.*), 118
Lebarty, lebberty: liberty, 113, 122
Ledyr: leather, 44
Leful: lawful, 65
Leiv: leave, 143
Letany: litany, 35
Lettl(e): little, 132, 138
Leuing: living, 65
Leuke-warme: lukewarm, 35
Leve(d): live(d), 23, 143
Levef: live (*vb.*), 122; leave (*vb.*), 122
Levenardys: (St.) Leonard's, 25
Leves: lives, 112
Levethe: liveth, 40

N

Nawnt(e): aunt, 48
Need: Ned, 117
Nempted: named, 29
Newe Castelle uppon Tynde: Newcastle-on-Tyne, 37
Newyr: never, 63
Nideth: needeth, 102
Nimlest: 'nimblest,' most swiftly, 97
Nonkilles: uncle's, 48
Norlache: Northleach, 67
Norwec(h)e: Norwich, 25, 40, 42
Noside: noised, 74
Nowembyr: November, 64
Nowntes: aunt's, 48
Nowth: not, not at all, 25
Noynne: noon, 54
Nues, nuse: news, 108, 110, 120
Nuw: new, 88
Nyght: nigh, 71

O

Obleged: obliged, 127
Obleigingly: obligingly, 124
Oboysauns: obeisance, 36
Oc(c)ation: occasion, 111, 116, 132
Offecers: officers, 79
Oithe: oath, 74
Okapy: occupy, use, 53
Old: hold, 48
Ollyness: holiness, 68
Omage: homage, 37, 38
Ombel: humble, 122
On: one, 41, 91
One: own, 100, 121, 126
Oon: one, an, 27, 30, 74, etc.
Oonlie, oonly: only, 27, 74
Openyon(e)(s): opinion(s), 128, 144
Opteyn: obtain, 76

Ordened: ordained, 70
Orderth: ordereth (3 *pl. indic.*), 71
Ore: our, 110
Ould: old, 90
Oulde: hold, 71
Oune: own, 47
Out: ought, 142
Ovar: over, 120
Owchesave: vouchsafe, 32
Owle: oil, 39
Ownly: only, 28
Owylle: oil, 92
Oyer: our, 25

P

Palys: palace, 50
Parceably: peaceably, 28
Parrsen; person, 123
Parswades: persuades, 133
Partriche, partyge, patridg, patridge(s): partridge(s), 106, 107, 114
Passayge: passage, 63
Patent: paten, 37
Pation: passion, 140
Patton: patent, 110
Pegyns, pejonys: pigeons, 38, 86
Pelere, pelore: pillory, 87, 93, etc.
Pepell, peple, pepull(e), pepylle: people, 34, 44, 50, 70, 78, 85, 108, etc.
Perdge: perch, 52
Perewks: perukes, 138
Perficcion: perfection, 107
Perfitlie: perfectly, 74
Pertaker: partaker, 110
Perticuller: particular, 126
Pervayle: prevail, 139
Pesse: piece, peace, 37, 85, 87
Petefully: pitifully, 88
Peteusle: piteously, 92

Reke: rick, 43

Remembret: remembreth, remember (*imper.*), 62

Resalefed: resolved, 122

Resayvyd: received, 58

Reselushons: resolutions, 122

Resorde: resort, 75

Resoullfe: resolve, 111

Respecks: respects, 116

Ressayve, resseyvid: received,
36, 53

Rether: rather, 143

Rewerent: reverend, 60

Rewlar: ruler, 67

Riatous: riotous, 31

Ribus: rebus, 148

Ritch: rich, 140

Riught: right, 63

Roberd: Robert, 107

Rooges: rogues, 120

Rook: rock, 78

Rouchester: Rochester, 35

Rowe: raw, 93

Ruight: right, 67

Ruing: ruin, 130

Rygth: right, 46, 47, 48, etc.

Ryscharde: Richard, 69

Rysse: rise, 85

Ryt: right, 68

Ryteings: writings, 114

Rythe(e), ryught: right (*sb. and
adj.*), 24, 32, 41, 63, etc.

S

Sade: said, 121

Salfe-garde: safeguard, 94

Salftye: safety, 94

Sallating: salading, the making
of salads, 138

Salve: salve or save, 105

Sargentys: sergeants, 38

Sartain(e)ly, sarten, sartyne:
certain(ly), 60, 86, 117, 131

Saruant: servant, 117

Sarued: served, 98

Sarues, saruis: service, 114,
115

Sarvaynte: servant, 57

Sarve: serve, 108

Sarves, sarvis: service, 106, 121

Satesfy, satisfy, 110

Savete: safety, 58

Savor, Savyr: Saviour, 77, 78

Sawe: save, 61

Sawle: soul, 46

Sayelles: sales, 61

Schaffold(e): scaffold, 34

Schardge: charge, 53

Scharlet: scarlet, 34

Scharsyte: scarcity, 38

Schaull: shall, 67

Sche: show, 63

Schelyngs: shillings, 38

Schepyt: shipped, 58

Scher: shire, 62

Schorderys: shoulders, 50

Schotlande: Scotland, 37

Schoyd: showed, 65

Schwld: should, 42

Schynys: chains, 34

Schyrte: shirt, 35

Scutyons: scutcheons, 140

Se(a)ke: seek, 98

Searuant, searue: servant,
serve, 116

Secler: secular, 65

Seell: sell, 61

Sekenesse: sickness, 25, 65

Sempyll: simple, single, 52

Sen: send, 42

Senc(e): since, 99, 128

Send(e): sent, 26, 27, 37, 57,
etc.

Sengyll, senkyll: single, 52

Sens: since, 82

Sent: saint, 25, 38; send, 54

Serchyd, sergyd: searched, 32

Serten: certain, 92

Servand(es), servauntts: ser-
vant(s), 87, 88, 92

Seth: saith, 72
Setts: sits, 145
Settyrday: Saturday, 59
Seurtie: surety, 28
Sevear(e): severe, 125, 130
Sewyr: sure, 63
Sexe: six, 41
Sey: saw, 42
Seynge: seeing, 30
Shar(s): share(s), 131
Shawynge: showing, 75
Shayres: shares, 111
Shep(p)e(s): ship(s), 86, 108
Sheppyd: shipped, 70
Sherars: sharers, 131
Shertys: shirts, 44
Shoes: shows, 126
Shott: shut, 79
Shoulders: soldiers, 117
Shouwed: showed, 119
Showyng: shoeing, 44
Shoyn: shoon, shoes, 45
Shrich: screech, 96
Shroyff-Monday: Shrove-Monday, 92
Shuer: sure, 123
Shurt(t)(e)(s): shirts, 79, 86
Sircut: circuit, 130
Skul: ability, 103
Sleept: slept, 135
Smothist: smoothest, 145
So(a)gars: soldiers, 144
Sobstons: substance, 60
Soker: succour, 80
Solders: soldiers, 108
Soles: souls, 123
Soomwhat: somewhat, 99
Soone: son, 110
Sophytiently: sufficiently, 129
Soposse: suppose, 48
Sor: swore, 38
Soster: sister('s), 62
Soudeours, souldeours: soldiers, 23
Soung: sung, 95
Spake: speak, 136

Spaw: spa, 127
Speand: spend, 127
Spekin: speaking, 142
Speelt: spelt, 146
Spende: spent, 44
Spilling: spelling, 149
Sqwyer: squire, 53
Sshuwlde: should, 42
Staitly: stately, 140
Stanche: staunch, 100
Standert: standard, 83
Stanes: Staines, 69
Stereth, steryd: stirreth, (-ed), 36, 81
Stiaminghot: steaming hot, 131
Stils: styles (*vb.*), 129
Stoan: stone, 143
Stoufe: stuff, 106
Straights: straits, 97
Strickly: strictly, 111
Stroynge: strong, or strange, 30
Sture(d), sturrid: stir(red), 24, 29, 98
Stwart, Stweard: (Lord) Steward, 134
Styll: decide, agree, 52
Subsete: subsidy, 58
Suffry: suffer (*infin.*), 47
Sugiorne: sojourn, 48
Sugsess: success, 115
Sunn: son, 107
Surte: surety, 48
Sutch: such, 131
Sutes: suits, 95
Suth: south, 77
Swche: such, 75
Sweathen: Sweden, 112
Swmme: some, 42
Swster: sister, 75
Syn: saint, 37

T

Taffata: taffeta, 35
Takinge: taken, 108

Talbose: Tallboys, 57
Tamsen: Thomasine, Thompson, 126
Tavarne: tavern, 93
Tell: till, 116, 134, 146
Teryn: tarry, 31
Thar: their, 122, 123; there, 128
Thawgh: though, 65
The: see *They*
Thechyng: teaching, 88
Ther: dare, 31
There: their, 125, 126
Thetcher: thatcher, 45
Thetchyng: thatching, 45
They: the (*and vice versa*), 37, 61, 127, etc.
Thim: them, 122
Thogth: though, 84
Those: these, 109
Thousant, thousens: thousand(s), 108, 128
Thousenth: thousandth, 128
Thrashold: threshold, 130
Threasorer: Treasurer, 104
Thress: thresh, 43
Threvoles: frivolous, 145
Throughts: throats, 120
Thruw: threw, 91
Till: tell, 121
Toar: tore, 140
Toing: towing, 134
Tooched: touched, 146
Toold: told, 114, 118
Tordis: towards, 122
Torke: Turk, 49
Torner: Turner, 129
Torter: torture, 143
Toshith: toucheth, 69
Toumes: tombs, 86
Towlde: told, 67
Traidys: tragedies, 147
Trauell: travail, labour, 95
Travaile: travel, 124
Trawthe: truth, 26; troth, 30
Treste: trust (*sb.*), 62

Trewthe: truth, 30
Trink: trunk, 148
Trouth: truth, 28; troth, 53
Trowst: trust (1 *sg. indic.*), 76
Trwste: trust, 63
Tuch: touch, 134
Tuysday: Tuesday, 26
Twchyng: touching, 32
Twitnam: Twickenham, 140
Tynggys: things, 42
Tyyll: tile, 74

Þ

þepartyd: departed, 62
þer: dare, 31

U

Undowyng: undoing, 28
Unsoffethe: unsought, 34
Untreuly: untruly, 47
Unusyell: unusual, 140
Uttmyst: utmost, 26

V (= [v] *and* [u])

Vacabundes, vacobondes: vagabonds, 83, 86
Vally de shamber: 'valet-de-chambre,' 136
Vallyed, valowe: value(d), 33, 141
Vant: vaunt, 97
Vary: very, 78
Vayage: voyage, 68
Vekeres: vicars, 83
Ventaros: venturous, 121
Venter: venture, 133
Veraly, verely: verily, 25, 41, 45, 59, etc.
Vnsweatests: unsweetest, 118
Voiolence: violence, 147
Vomett: vomit, 92
Vowchesaf: vouchsafe, 42
Voyne: vine, 77

Vwchesave: vouchsafe, 32
Vyssyones: visions, 87

W

Wake: week (a for [ɛ] or [ɛi]), 116
Walkin: walking, 131
Wallde: would, 68
War(e): were, 70, 72, 120
Warled: world, 58
Warke: work, 81
Wars: worse, 65, 82
Water: Walter, 62
Wayse: wise, 71
Weake: week, 117
Wear(e): were, 108, 114, 115, 126, etc.
Weche: which, 39, 40, 47, etc.
Wechesafe: vouchsafe, 40
Weell: well, 61, 117
Weete: wheat, 43
Wekid: wicked, 65
Well: will, 62, 106
Wellffete: velvet, 57
Wensday(s): Wednesday(s),96, 140
Wente: weened, 66
Wenter: winter, 70, 108
Wenyge: weening, 34
Werce: worse, 26
Wery: weary, 27; very, 71
Wexe: wax, 100
Weytte: weight, 25
Whalew: value, 63
Whar: war, 60
Whas: was, 60
Whay: way, 67
Whe: we, 60, 63, 68, etc.
Whekes: weeks, 68
Whelde: would, 63
Whell: well, 63
Whept: wept, 88
Wher(e): were, 63, 67, 88
Whery: very, 68

Whin: when, 121
Whisse: wise, way, 60
Whith: white, 78
Whither: whether, 133
Whollde: would, 60, 63
Whor: were, 63
Whorlld: world, 60
Whos: was, 63, 67, 68, etc.
Whot: what, 127, 130
Who(w)l(l)de: would, 63, 67
Whythe: with, 34
Wiesses: vices, 113
Wike: week, 81
Wilfar: welfare, 24
Will: well, 122
Willcom: welcome, 120
Wirship: worship, 66
Wis(s), wis(s)ed, wishse: wish(ed), 113, 115, 121
Witsafe: vouchsafe, 84
Wndyrstonde: understand, 63, 68
Wochesaf(e): vouchsafe, 25, 39
Wod: would, 129, 130
Woke: week (see OED, *s.v.* 'Week,' a common form in XVth and XVIth century
Wolfully: wilfully, 74
Won(e)(s): one(s), 122, 123, 133, etc.
Woold: would, 87
Woolfe: wolf, 91
Woork: work, 96
Woorthy: worthy, 95
Worchepfwl: worshipful, 41
Worll: world, 62
Worly: worldly, 46
Wos: was, 120
Wosshyng: washing, 44
Wrack: wreck, 95
Wraste: wrest, 82
Wrethe: writ, 62
Wretten, wretyn: written, 32, 39, 40, 42, 61, etc.
Wriet, wright, wryght: write, 60, 67, 122